Fairness

Fairness

Theory & Practice of Distributive Justice

Nicholas Rescher

Transaction Publishers
New Brunswick (U.S.A.) and London (U.K.)

Copyright © 2002 by Transaction Publishers, New Brunswick, New Jersey.

All rights reserved under International and Pan-American Copyright Conventions. No part of this book may be reproduced or transmitted in any form or by any means, electronic or mechanical, including photocopy, recording, or any information storage and retrieval system, without prior permission in writing from the publisher. All inquiries should be addressed to Transaction Publishers, Rutgers—The State University, 35 Berrue Circle, Piscataway, New Jersey 08854-8042.

This book is printed on acid-free paper that meets the American National Standard for Permanence of Paper for Printed Library Materials.

Library of Congress Catalog Number: 2002075264
ISBN: 0-7658-0110-8
Printed in Canada

Library of Congress Cataloging-in-Publication Data

Rescher, Nicholas
  Fairness : theory & practice of distributive justice / Nicholas Rescher.
    p. cm.
  Includes bibliographical references and index.
  ISBN 0-7658-0110-8 (alk. paper)
  1. Distributive justice. 2. Wealth—Moral and ethical aspects. 3. Fairness.
I. Title.

HB835 .R455 2002
172'.2—dc21   2002075264

For John Haldane

Contents

Acknowledgements	vii
Preface: Distributive Justice	ix
1. A Look Ahead	ix
2. The Task of a Theory of Distributive Justice	xi
1. Treating Claims Impartially	1
1. Claims and Their Basis	1
2. Fair Shares	9
3. Fairness and Advantage	13
4. Fair Division	15
5. Equality before the State	17
6. Impartiality	21
2. Abstract Fairness and Claim Proportionality	25
1. Strict Fairness	25
2 Two Basic Principles	28
3. On Objectivity: Strict Fairness is not Subjective	30
4. Fairness and Procedural Appropriateness	32
5. Allocating Fair Shares	34
6. Randomness: A Last Resort	36
7. Egalitarian Justifications of Proportionality in Distribution	38
8. Negativities	39
9. Different Sorts of Claims	40
3. The Liabilities and Assets of Fairness	45
1. Fairness Does not Seek Popularity nor Honor Power	45
2. Distributive Desiderata	46
3. A Variety of Allocation Principles	50
4. Indivisible Goods Need not Defeat Fairness	51
5. Fairness Can Accommodate Shortfalls and Windfalls	52

4. Going Beyond Fairness? Subjective Equity and Benevolent Allocation ... 55
   1. Subjective Evaluation and Pragmatic Equity ... 55
   2. Subjective Equity and Paternalism ... 59
   3. Paternalistic Benevolence in Distribution: The Advantages of Allocation by Max-Value Equity ... 62
   4. Further Examples ... 68
   5. Negativities ... 74
   6. Unreasonable and/or Deceptive Valuations ... 76
   7. Affective Involvement ... 77
   8. A Lesson ... 79

5. Probabilistic Expectations: Dividing Prospective Gains in Risk Situations: The Historical Background ... 81
   1. Expectations Generalized ... 84
   2. The Leibniz-Keynes Doctrine ... 86
   3. The Problem of Adequacy ... 88

6. Predominantism: Limits of Proportionism in Pre-Ownership ... 91
   1. Proportionalism vs. Predominance ... 91
   2. A Historical Interlude ... 95
   3. Leibniz and Keynes at Sea? ... 97
   4. Why Predominantism in Ownership Cases ... 98
   5. The Lesson ... 101

7. Dividing Credit for Discoveries: Limits of Proportionalism in Teamwork ... 103
   1. Distributive vs. Collective Cooperation ... 103
   2. Principles of Credit Allocation ... 106
   3. Fairness Sustained ... 108

8. The Pragmatic Rationale of Distribution Principles ... 111
   1. Epistemic vs. Moral Credit/Discredit ... 111
   2. A Difference of Aims ... 115
   3. A Look at the Law ... 117
   4. Further Perspectives ... 118
   5. The Big Picture: Functionalistic Pragmatism ... 120

Bibliography ... 125

Name Index ... 133

Acknowledgements

Over the years since my 1966 book on *Distributive Justice* the issues of this domain have continued to intrigue me and give rise to further relevant publications. (The bibliography at the end of this book provides the relevant data.) However, the proximate cause of the present book was reading *Fair Division* by Steven J. Brams and Alan D. Taylor (Cambridge: Cambridge University Press, 1996). This interesting foray into mathematical division techniques seems to me to fall into difficulty because of an insufficient recognition that appropriate practice in this domain must be grounded by moral and ethical principles, and that such principles cannot be left out of sight if it is actually *fairness* that is the object of our concern. These authors, along with most economists and decision theorists, seek to separate the concept of fairness from the province of ethics and moral philosophy. But this approach invites misunderstandings and distortions which the present book seeks to put right in an effort to recover the concept of fairness for the normative domain where it belongs.

The book was written in Pittsburgh, primarily during the 2000-2001 academic year, although in part it draws on work of earlier years. I acknowledge with appreciation the encouragement and counsel I have received from Professor Irving Louis Horowitz. And I am grateful to Estelle Burris for her able and patient efforts in producing a word-processed manuscript suitable for the printer's needs.

Nicholas Rescher
Pittsburgh PA
November 2000

Preface: Distributive Justice

1. A Look Ahead

This book is a study in distributive justice whose mission is to clarify the conception of fair shares by elucidating and explaining the principles that are at issue here. Its principal aim is to free the concept of fairness from various misunderstandings and confusions by showing how its definitively characteristic features prevent its absorption by such related conceptions as paternalistic benevolence, radical egalitarianism, or social harmonization. To accomplish this, it is necessary to avoid various confusions arising from the economists' penchant for individual preferences, from the decision theorists' concern for averting envy, and from the political theorists sympathies for egalitarianism. The object is to recover the concept of fairness and its rooting in ethical theory by highlighting its fundamentally moral concern for matters closer to justice and natural law than to economics or conflict resolution. Accordingly, the book's central thesis is that fairness is a fundamentally ethical conception whose distinctive modus operandi contrasts sharply with the aims of paternalism, preference-maximization, or economic advantage.

The following theses will be substantiated in the course of this inquiry:

1. The idea of distributive equity forms the core of the concept of fairness in matters of distributive justice. The coordination of shares with valid claims is the crux here.

2. The appropriate pursuit of fairness requires *objective* rather than *subjective* evaluation of the goods being shared out.

3. Fairness is therefore something quite different from subjective equity as based on the personal evaluation of distributive goods by the claimants involved.

x   **Fairness**

4. Insofar as subjective equity is a concern—and thus insofar as the issue is one of plausible economics rather than strict justice—the appropriate procedure for its realization is a process of maximum-value distribution.

5. In matters of distributive justice, the distinction between ownership creation and preexisting ownership is pivotal and calls for proceeding on very different principles in these two cases.

6. The principles of procedure that are appropriate in matters of distributive justice are context dependent. And their validating rationale is pragmatic in that it pivots the differential requisites for achieving efficacy and effectiveness in realizing the characteristic aims and purposes of the sort of distribution that is at issue.

Viewed in this perspective, fairness is a concept whose reason for being lies in the area of impartial justice rather than in the perhaps no less important but nevertheless more crass and mundane domain of human satisfactions. And the dialectic between what is advantageous and what is right, fairness is something that is geared far more closely to the latter than to the former. Accordingly, one of the main objectives of the book is to reclaim fairness for the ethics of distributive justice, recapturing it from those economists who have seized it as a means for fostering their own purposes relating to the efficiency of distributions. Fairness, so it is argued, is a value that belongs rather to justice than to economics.

Moreover, such an approach sees it, fairness is an inherently *functional* conception: it has a purposive role—a job to do. This job is the preservation of harmony and good feeling in a group of such claimants through the fact that when any good (or bad) is being allocated none can (reasonably) feel aggrieved as the victim of unjust treatment. Not that all are treated alike and receive equal shares, but rather that all are treated in the same way—according to the uniform application of generally appliable principles which have a cogent rationale of justification.

The pivotal issue for distributive justice is not the historical question of who came by what how in the past, but the present-oriented issue of whether what is being allocated to people here and now is in line with the established and currently prevailing principles of claim-establishment—principles which, of course, have a history that is now beyond unravelling. Distributions, like journeys, must begin from where we are.

2. The Task of a Theory of Distributive Justice

The idea that legitimate claims must be honored as fundamental to justice encompasses both the major sectors of this domain. For when those claims *are claims of ours*, we have to do with rights, while when the issue is one of heeding the *claims of others* we have to do with *obligations*.

The theory of social justice at large confronts the task elucidating how to determine the appropriate claims of individuals. And the theory of specifically distributive justice addresses the task of claim settlement, of allocating the shares of relevantly available resources in light of these claims. The deliberations of this book focus upon this second set of issues. Presuming a matter of claim determination to be settled, it addresses the problem of realizing to the greatest possible extent a distribution that renders to each claimant a "fair and proper share" of the good (or evil) at issue.

The present inquiry seeks to elucidate what is at issue in one important aspect of justice, namely fairness. The elucidation of this concept and the exploration of its *modus operandi* is the cardinal aim of the book. What is at issue here is not simply a matter of word juggling—of considering what is at issue in calling a distribution "fair." We are not engaged in a merely lexicographic exercise. For fairness represents a deeply normative-evaluative conception whose application matters a great deal to how people think and act regarding one another. It plays a significant role in law in public policy, in administration, and in everyday life. Whether we are prepared to characterize the people about us as acting in ways that are fair or otherwise crucially conditions how we judge and thereby how we treat them.

Getting clear on just what fairness involves is accordingly not a matter of lexicography but of looking at the sort of work for which the concept is instituted. And in the end, this task cannot be hopelessly difficult. After all, even young children have an acute sense of the issue. Exclamations like "That's not fair!" and "Now it's my turn!" are prominent among the familiar cries of the playground. A sense of fairness is a basic human reality, manifested even by the youngest. From our earliest days we are naturally indignant at unfairness—and especially so when we ourselves are its victim.

What marks fairness as a fundamentally moral concept is the consideration that in general we would unhesitatingly (and rightly) reprehend someone who acted in a deliberately unfair way. Of course, the nature of the transgression—and in particular its motivation—will make a decisive difference here. Did the agent act out of selfishness, out of prejudice, or in a misguided attempt to balance out a past unfairness? The degree of reprehension will differ throughout such cases. But even where it is small, the fact that unfairness involves moral culpability invariably remains.

It is not surprising that we owe to the juridically minded Romans some of the most acute insights into the nature of justice, since this is among the more legalistic of ethical concepts. However, for this very reason it does not constitute an ultimate factor in ethics. A juster world is not necessarily a morally optimal one: in an emphasis on justice there is a somewhat carping insistence on giving and getting "one's due share" that ignores the dimension of generosity, sacrifice, self-abnegation, and deeds of supererogation. From an ethical standpoint, the dispensation of justice has something of the Old Testament air of an insistence upon bare essentials. The result is that philosophical writers on the ethics of distribution traditionally contrast *justice* with *benevolence*, recognizing that the line of division is not perfectly sharp, because, as Sidgwick put it, there is a "borderland, tenented with expectations which are not quite claims and with regard to which we do not feel sure whether Justice does or does not require us to satisfy them."[1] This distinction will have to figure prominently in the setting of cogent deliberations regarding fairness.

One of the main lessons that emerges from the deliberations of the book is that a concept like fairness (and doubtless also its cousins in political economic, and legal thought) rest on rather straightforward basic principles whose applicative implementation amidst the complexities of the real world can turn out to involve rather long and complicated stories. For while distributive fairness in the abstract is a relatively simple idea, its operation amidst the staggering diversity of situations that arise in quotidian life can come to be a very complicated business. Its heed of the distinctions and caveats that will accordingly arise with respect to fair distributions make the book as much a critique as a defense of fairness, in that the complexities involved in a sensible and rational implementation of fairness bring to view the limitations to its dogmatically simpleminded application. This may not be a lesson that people want to hear in this era of ideologically motivated oversimplification, but its validity means that it is unquestionably a point that philosophers have an ex officio obligation to urge.

Note

1. Henry Sidgwick, *The Methods of Ethics,* 7th edition (London: Macmillan, 1907), p. 270.

1

Treating Claims Impartially

(1) People's claims are substantially a matter of social reality: of positive law, usage, custom, and the like. (2) And fairness strictly construed, consists in allocating shares in mathematical proportion with claims. (3-4) Fairness is emphatically not a matter of honoring the preferences of people. Rather, it is an instrumentality of justice, and so not of social utility or public welfare. (5) The issue of "equality before the state" is something complex that actually stops well short of a literalistic egalitarianism. (6) However, procedural impartiality is a crucial aspect of fairness.

1. Claims and Their Basis

One speaks in matters of distributive justice of dividing "goods," but this term is actually a sort of shorthand for "goods and bads." Any adequate theory of this domain has to be able to deal with negativities as readily as positivities.

Distributive justice pivots crucially on the existence of claims. For as Aristotle emphasized long ago, what is involved here is "a kind of proportion" (*analogon ti*) where the shares of those involved are in alignment with one another "according to desert" (*kat' axian*).[1] A claim represents what an individual claimant ought "by rights" to obtain, and where the aspect of justice is absent, there are no claims either. It is sometimes said that "what is bad about inequality is its unfairness."[2] But this pious sentiment is very much of an exaggeration that needs to be carefully qualified. For only when there is a preexisting equality of valid claims is an inequality of distribution bad, unreasonable, or unfair. There is nothing unfair about it when the victor of the race gets a prize but the losers a mere commendation for good effort. There is nothing unfair about it if the worker gets a wage and the onlooker nothing. There is nothing unfair about it if the ship's captain with his great responsibilities gets a large salary and the cabin boy a modest wage. For the fact of it is that the claims of these differently situated individuals are themselves very different.

Claims are something significantly distinct from deserts. People do not necessarily *deserve* that which they can lay a legitimate claim to. If I hire you at a wage more than your services are worth you may not deserve to have the salary you earn, but you nevertheless have a valid claim to it. Again, you may not deserve to win the lottery, but having done so you and you alone have a legitimate claim to the prize.

Someone's having a claim upon something is certainly a good reason for giving it to him (albeit not invariably a decisive one). But the converse does not hold since not every good reason for giving is linked to a claim. There are many reasons to give something to someone—roses to one's beloved, say, or a birthday gift to a friend—that do not correspond to an actual *claim* of any sort.

Consider two analogous but actually very different cases:

I. A man is beset by some beggars in the street. He gives a dollar to one and nothing to the rest.

II. A charitable foundation is besieged by a variety of worthy causes for support. It chooses to support one but not the others.

In the first case, the nonbeneficiary has no just cause for complaint. For in this example there are no actual claims at issue: the beggars have wants and needs, but no claims. None of these supplicants has a right to any support at all; all of them lack any claims for consideration by the chooser, and in the absence of any claims upon him this benefactor is under no obligation in the matter. He can indulge his whims arbitrarily without liability to warranted recrimination. His treatment of those beggars is unequal but not unfair. Where there are no claims they cannot be dishonored. But the second case is quite different. As a recognized public charity with a duly encorporated mission and with corresponding public benefits (e.g., in point of taxation) bestowed upon it, a foundation is obligated to treat its would-be beneficiaries as per the merits of their substantiating case for support as per the terms of its charter. So here justice and fairness are definitely part of the picture.

It is also important to distinguish between a *claim* and an *entitlement* in relation to matters of distribution. The former—an individual's claim—is the amount that an individual can justifiably hold to be his or her due in the absence of competing claims upon the limited amount available for distribution. The latter—entitlement—is the individual's share *after* all such relevant considerations have been taken into due account. Thus let it be that X dies leaving behind an estate of $600 but also debts to three creditors who are owed $300 each. Then each of these creditors indeed has a claim to $300, but ends up being entitled to only $200 of it. The claim is what the creditor can demand at the start of a process of just division; the entitlement is the claimant's just due as determined at its end (if it proceeds appropriately). The point is that a claim represents what an individual ought *ideally* to be given in light of the principles of justice, while that individual's entitlement is what they ought to be given *in the circumstances*—which may wind up being something rather different.

But where do claims come from: how are they constituted? This is not a matter of abstract general principle. Instead, the claims of individuals are rooted in the operative ground rules of the society that constitutes their existential context.

The legally mandated inheritance claims of individuals differ from one country (or even state) to another, as do their obligations in matters of taxation or military service. Can you lay claim to the apples that fall on your property from you neighbor's tree? This is not a matter of universal abstract justice but of the local custom and legal ordinances. Claims generally hinge upon law, usage, and custom rather than upon theoretical general principles of ethics by themselves. The yield of agricultural land is customarily divided 50:50 between the landowner and his tenant farmers. In the case of bankruptcy, the unsecured creditors all get so much on the dollar by proportionate shares. Movie theater seats are usually made available to the public on a first-come first-serve basis but symphony concert seats are generally contracted for. You pay for a restaurant meal after the event but for a movie before. Only with the largest issues of life, liberty, and opportunity are your claims matters of universal human rights at large; for the most part they will depend on the laws and conventions of particular contexts, and reflect the relevant legal, social, and political realities. In the USA, no elector's fair share of voting power is diminished by the fact that states of small population have just as great representation in the Senate as states of large population do. Nor does the disenfranchisement of under-age voters—which legally sets their voting claims at naught—mean that their exclusion from the voting booth is unfair.

Consider the following situation: A boatload of survivors settle a deserted island. Ground rules of obligations and rights, of duty and ownership are established, by hook or crook, in the resultant community that ultimately establishes a stable order to which people on the whole give acquiescence and acceptance. And then a second boatload of newcomers arrives. How are they to be fitted in? What are their fair shares of rights, privileges, duties, entitlements, and obligations?

There is simply no answer to this question that can be validated on the basis of theoretical general principles. The clock has to be turned back to zero. The historic process of forging a moral order has to be resumed. There is no abstract reason why these newcomers have to be content with what the old order has assigned to them—viz., nothing. There is no abstract reason why the old settlers have to accept the newcomers on the basis of one-person, one-share equality under the old rules. A new order has to be evolved in which people-in-general are willing to acquiesce. And this sort of resolution is not theoretical but developmental. The outcome is not so much a social contract as a social settlement. What people will—and should—get is not so much what they deserve on the basis of theoretical general principles—the world does not, cannot work like that! What they will—and should—get is what the sedimented stabilization of social process attributes to them. Here the only pathway to social practice leads through the brambles of social history. (But, of course, the process will have the coloration of justice only when the people involved are rational—that is, do not, in the absence of good reasons, overreadily acquiesce in arrangements that are contrary to their interests.)

Claims are usually created by concrete arrangements rather than abstract principles. Consider the distribution of public offices—the governorship of states, say—in line with elections with the usual winner-take-all allocation. The claims of the less successful candidate—however strong—are set as naught. The candidate who loses to his opponent by a margin of 40:60 does not get to fill the office 40 percent of the time. In effect, the winner of the election has a claim on the office whose weight is decisive in contrast with the loser's claim of zero weight. In Roman law, all eligible heirs share equally in the case of an intestate decedent. (The reason for this is apparently to be found in the old, original custom of co-ownership of all members of a family in the family property, the paterfamilias being seen rather as the administrator than the owner.[3]) But most law-systems treat the claims of differently related individuals differently in such a situation. Users of the postal system who have franked their letter feel equally entitled to the delivery service irrespective of whether the letter is going across the town or across the country. But users of the telephone system do not (at least as yet) claim an equality of entitlement irrespective of the distance involved. The cost of subway transportation in New York is distance-invariant, but in London's underground distance is a key factor in pricing journeys. Assessing the comparative size of claims is less a matter of theory than one of social reality: of positive law, usage, custom, and the like. For example, consider the case of people who pile dirt and debris against a wall that collapses in consequence. Here liability for the costs of repair are allocated proportionately by amount (by weight rather than volume), unless each separate contribution is of itself sufficient to produce collapse, in which case the liability is divided 50:50, irrespective of the weight of contributions.[4]

This comparative size of claims is, of course, a pivotal factor. When goods (and bads) cannot be evaluated and compared with one another—somehow, by hook or crook—then there is no prospect of implementing the idea of fairness in matters of this distribution.[5]

It is, of course, crucial that claims be set in order with objective, or at least neutrally impartial standards. People must be systematically precluded from any prospect of unmerited benefit by unduly exaggerating their claims. The old Roman legal maxim, *ex turpi causa non oritur actio*, applies here in the construction of "no valid claim arises through an improper act."

The key idea of procedural fairness lies in the injunction "Treat people differently only in cases where there is a difference that actually makes a difference in some contextually appropriate regard." For only when this condition is satisfied is there a rationale—a reasonable justification—for that difference in treatment. Of course, that phrase "contextually appropriate regard" takes us into the matter of the *purposive context* of the procedural domain at issue. A training program can, without unfairness, discriminate between those who have an aptitude for the activity at issue (talent for a sport or a musical instrument) but to discriminate on grounds of race or sex would be inappropriate and thus unfair. The committee awarding a best-actor award can—indeed should—discriminate on the basis of quality or performance but the age of those involved will—or should—be irrelevant. A scholarship being awarded "to enhance student-body diversity" can, without unfairness, take race into account, but one that is awarded "to recognize the most improved student" cannot. The purposive context of a distribution represents a critical factor for the issue of procedural fairness. (And, of course, some purposes can be inherently unfair of themselves—"ethnic cleansing," for one.)

Claims are accordingly context-dependent. In families, small children establish claims on their parents by need; performance is pretty much irrelevant. In business, on the other hand, employees establish claims on their employers by performance, and here need is pretty much irrelevant. But in each case the nature of the enterprise is the crucial determinant. Families survive and thrive through mutual care; businesses survive and thrive through making profits. Claims generally serve their legitimacy through social arrangements dictated by functional efficacy relative to context.

Whether the societally established practices regarding claims is prudent or socially beneficial and duly recognizant of people's best interests are certainly legitimate issues. But not whether the socially established practices regarding claims are fair. For claims determine fairness and not the other way around.

One deep-rooted difficulty with respect to fairness arises with the question of who is to count a claimant. In U.S. governance, states are treated as claimants in regard to representation in the Senate but individuals in regard to representation in the House. This sort of thing, of course, leads to complications because custom, law, and social practice once more become operative factors. Accordingly, within any society there are generally established practice institutions, customs, laws, rules, and the like, that determine matters of rights, claims, and entitlements. And these are matters that people have by and large come to terms with and have come to accept as appropriate and just. (One would hope—and to some extent expect—that if this were not so those arrangements would have been changed by now.) A viable society needs stable rules and we should suppose that its members on the whole acquiesce in the prevailing order of things as sufficiently just for practical purposes—not ideal, perhaps, but tolerable and acceptable. At any rate we shall, for our present purposes, assume that it is so.

This sort of thing is unavoidable because where claims are concerned considerations of abstract general principle simply cannot decide everything. Consider an example. Two states share a frontier along a river upon which each needs to draw water for industrial and agricultural use. How is the river water to be divided between them? They turn to an impartial arbitrator to make a fair division. What factor should this arbiter fix on to serve as a proportionality basis: population, irrigation-requiring farmland, water-requiring enterprises, or some combination of the above? And if one state uses its water allocation very efficiently (via purification and recycling facilities, for example), while the other state is wasteful should this be taken into account with one state rewarded and the other penalized? It is impossible to give an answer in general principle here. All that can be said is that the just arbiter will take some not inappropriate account of every significantly relevant factor. And if he fails to do so, he is being not just unfair but unreasonable and, indeed, incompetent.

In any event, the nowadays fashionable idea that claims are grounded in an originating social contract of some sort is highly problematic. There are two ways to construe the idea of such a contract: the historically realistic and the hypothetical. But the former option is spurious: the idea of a social contract as an actual historical eventuation is a mere fiction (apart from a handful of cases such as the launching of the Swiss confederation). And the second option will have to pivot on what the society *ought* to endorse contractually—what it would, if rational, consent to contracting for. But in this case we might as well short-cut the social contract and ask what is rational directly. So in this case the "social contract" idea becomes redundant and dispensable.

To be sure, some contemporary justice theorists approach the matter of claim validation via the question of what sorts of claim-structure would be initiated by ideally rational agents designing a socio-legal order *de novo* and *in vacuo*. But this, of course, is obviously unrealistic pie in the sky. Such abstract idealization is simply not on the agenda of real-world concerns. The reality of it is that here we are emplaced *in medias res* within an existing and functioning socio-legal order. Of course this order is something that we can criticize and endeavor to change. But any effective efforts along these lines will unavoidably have to be channeled through the political processes in place—or, barring that, consigned to the uncertain arbitrament of the streets and the barricades. Here, as elsewhere, we have no plausible and realistic alternative to starting the journey from just exactly where we are—and where we are with this issue is a matter of emplacement in a setting that has its claim-justifying and claim-altering processes firmly in place. And even if we do not like the *status quo*, we must deal with it within the conditions and circumstances of the moment.

But are established claims always appropriate for the determination of fairness? What of primogeniture, or of male-only eligibility for voting or for the ownership of real property? Are established practices always fair and just. Of course not. But where custom-endorsed claims are unjustified and inappropriate it is because they are dislodged by larger and weightier claims of even greater standing. For valid claims, however weak, can only be displaced by other claims.

The rational validation of a claim accordingly is not simply a matter of its conformity to social practice: here too the real need not automatically be normatively appropriate. For validation there must additionally be good reason to think that the practice at issue is one that redounds, on balance, to the advantage of the group as a whole in the setting of its prevailing circumstances.

Determining claims can be complicated. A wealthy man dies, leaving a will that gives 100 shares of stock X to A and 100 shares of stock Y to B. Now on the day the will was drafted, stock X stood at $40 per share and stock Y at $20. It seems fair to conclude that the testator intended to have A twice the amount he was leaving to B. But when the time comes for the estate actually to be divided among the heirs, the situation is very different. Stock X stands at $20 and stock Y at $40. No doubt A will advance a claim on the basis of the value of the testator's initial allocations and B will advance a claim on the basis of the explicit specifications of the will. In law, the latter claim will unquestionably prevail. But the ethical situation looks rather different in this regard because intent is here relevant—and indeed paramount. We have, in effect, a conflict between the legal and ethical claims and need to decide on the basis of contextual considerations which is to prevail.

An interesting case that has been discussed in the literature is this. A squad of twelve soldiers is engaged as volunteers on a dangerous mission. In the course of pursuing this, one of them must be chosen for an even greater risk—a dangerous reconnaissance, say. It is known that one of them has a special talent for the task. Is it fair that this person should be chosen? Or should the task be assigned on a random basis because equal claims are at issue?[5]

The answer is that it all depends on the exact nature of the case. Ordinarily, with all else equal and in the absence of special factors, all twelve soldiers, of course, have an equal claim on "being guarded against risks" and in this circumstance random selection is indeed the fair procedure. But suppose that the safety of the whole group depends on the success of that reconnaissance, and that its failure would endanger everyone. Then clearly the claims of the more talented for exemption from extra risk become substantially diminished. The right to security of that talented scout is now not unaffected but actually diminished by the comparable rights of his fellows. As is generally the case, the details of the context become a determinative factor.

In general, claims have an ultimately *functional* basis. If students are being selected for the award of a mathematical prize or if young violinists are being auditioned for a scholarship to a music conservatory, only the best has a claim to appointment. To give the place to another is the epitome of unfairness. And in all such cases, it is the aim or telos of the process of allocation that determines the existence and the magnitudes of the relevant claims.

In any case, the present deliberations will take claims as a given and proceed from there. Considerations of fairness proceed from a prior determination of appropriate claims and entitlements. The pivotal question now becomes: Those claims being as they are, where do we go from here?

2. Fair Shares

Fairness arises in two contexts, namely fairness-to and fairness-that. Doing something can be fair (or unfair) *to* a particular individual or group. (For example, it is not fair to Tom to charge him more than Bob for the same service; and it is not fair to women to pay them less for doing the same work.) Moreover, it can be fair (or unfair) that something be done by way of an individual not on general practice. (For example, it is not fair that Tom should be charged more than Bob for the same service, and it is not fair that women should be paid less than men for doing the same work.) However, fairness-to is more fundamental than fairness-that. Whenever it is unfair that something-or-other should happen, there will and must be individuals to whom this practice is unfair. Fairness at its basis is something that affects people through the fact that failing to abide by its demands inflicts inappropriate imposition on the legitimate rights and claims of individuals.

To get a clear grasp on what is at issue with fairness, it is a good idea to begin with unfairness. What sorts of considerations are at issue when people complain of unfair treatment in the allocations of goods? Three types of complaints will predominate here:

1. "I didn't get what I deserved."

2. "I lost out because of favoritism to X."

3. "They treated me 'by the book' but bent the rules for the others."

The corresponding factors involved are:

1. *Equity*. Having people's shares be proportionate to their claims. (And accordingly giving them equal shares in the case of equal claims.)

2. *Impartiality*. Avoiding favoritism and treating claimants with even-handedness—"without fear or favor."

3. *Uniformity*. Proceeding via the uniform application of appropriate principles. According everyone the privilege of "due process."

There may, of course, be a decisive reason for not giving someone that to which they have a legitimate claim. Suppose Uncle John's will leaves Cousin Robert $1,000. But when the uncle dies his estate comes to only $1,500 and his will also puts Cousin Ronald in exactly the same situation as Robert. Robert indeed has a legitimate claim to $1,000, but a conscientious and just executor will not give it to him—even though he can—because then like cases would not be treated alike.

Accordingly, the fair shares that represent one's actual entitlements are not the same as claims. Nevertheless, fair shares pivot on claims—in fact, fairness hinges critically on the comparative magnitude of the claims that are at issue in relation to the magnitude of the good being divided. This circumstance endows fairness with an abstract and formalistic character. For while claims arise from substantive considerations regarding established practices, their fair accommodation is a structural and procedural issue. (The only other factor required for fair resolutions is the amount and nature of the positivity or negativity that is to be distributed.)

Equity in distributive contexts is a matter of proportionality to *appropriate* claims. And this fact that fairness hinges on potentially arguable claims means that while there is not much room for disagreement about what *fairness* is, people will often disagree about *what is fair*. The complexity of claims means that questions of fairness will ultimately depend on the concrete details of the situation.

Take an example: the fairness of parents vis-à-vis children. Given that other things are equal, each child has an equivalent claim on the parents, it is clear that the interests of fairness require an equal allocation of such resources as time, attention and concern, effort and energy, and so on. Of course other things may not be equal. A sickly child will require and deserve more care and thus more parental time and expenditure, a handicapped child more attention and help, an unusually able child more encouragement and instruction, and so on. In the manner of these examples there will be various circumstances in which *need* becomes a primary factor in the establishment of claims—specifically in "paternalistic" circumstances.

Often a fixed quantity of a good or bad is at issue and sharing out is a zero-sum process: what one claimant gets must be taken away from others. Often—but by no means always. When many people collaborate in doing something heroic, they are all heroes and not just insignificant contributors. In sharing out penalties for a crime it is not that there is a fixed amount of penalty (fifty years for manslaughter, five years for auto theft) that is then somehow divided among the culprits so that teamwork becomes less risky for individuals.

But what happens in the case of conflicting claims? Uncle Ebenezer is no longer all that sharp when he writes his will. In one paragraph he leaves all of the contents of his library to cousin *A*. In another he leaves his entire collection of clocks to cousin *B*. Unfortunately, one of his precious clocks is in the library. Who is to get it? To all superficial appearances, both *A* and *B* are fully entitled to it. But in the circumstance we have to treat these claims as equal and opposite. One way or another, the value at issue has to get divided.

Again, two nations have a border dispute over a certain unpopulated and economically insignificant region. They ask the king of Ruritania to arbitrate and he appoints a commission to do the work. The commission decides that the first rival has a better historic claim to one sub-region and the other to another, leaving only a third sub-region of K square kilometers where the claim of the two rivals are equal. Presumably the division should then be made in such a way that (1) each claimant gets all of that well-entitled sub-region and half of that problematic sub-region, and (2) that the division of the latter should be effected in such a way that the resultant border between the two countries be as short as possible. The first condition serves the interests of fairness. And the second condition serves the interests of utility—or common sense, if you prefer—because (other things being equal) this condition optimizes a country's ease of access to its terrain. (This too could be seen as an aspect of fairness, since a country is presumably entitled not just to terrain but to conveniently accessible terrain.)

Again, Hare and Tortoise are to collaborate on a 50:50 basis in getting a message from point 1 to point 2. What is the fair division of labor? Is the journey of each to take the same time or cover the same distance? X and Y are to restock Z's refrigerator on a share-and-share-alike basis. Is each to contribute the same number of items or is to be items coming to be same aggregate cost? Such questions pose the issue of fairness in the face of items of multiparametric value (weight vs. cost, time vs. effort, and the like). This too is a substantive issue that will depend on the nature of the case.

Fairness, then, is a matter of the suitable honoring of appropriate claims. Specifically, in matters of division, it requires allocations to be made proportionately to the strength of the claims at issue. However, these claims need not be claims to goods or to money. Very different resources can be at issue. Fairness involves the equitable distribution of material and immaterial resources alike. And in an indirect way, the claimants need not be *persons*. In the allocation of manpower to scientific research, different problem areas have claim proportionate to the interest and importance of the problems at issue. In view of their status as such, guests of honor have the right to expect a greater-than-ordinary share of attention and consideration from their hosts. Again, in view of the expectations of its purchasers and users, the topics treated in an encyclopedia deserve an amount of space proportionate to their inherent importance, and the disasters reported in newspapers have a claim to prominence and volume to coverage proportionate to the damage and carnage involved. In such cases, saying of something impersonal like a topic in a curriculum or a problem-area of investigation that it is being shortchanged and treated unfairly is always to speak figuratively. At bottom, it is always a matter of how people are being treated as consuming or producing stakeholders in that topic or research area. Strictly speaking, only people can be treated fairly or unfairly, and not impersonal agencies.

3. Fairness and Advantage

Many authors talk as though there were no difference between fairness and distributive equality. But this equivalence is, in fact, something that obtains only in a very special circumstances, namely the case of equivalent or equal claims. And here the equal treatment of people when every relevant condition is equal is not so much a matter of justice as one of mere rationality. For rationality insists upon the "principle of sufficient reason" that when cases—of any sort—are treated differently there should be a cogent reason for doing so.

Fairness, at bottom, is a matter of equity of process—of dividing goods or bads on the basis of general principles that pertain to everyone alike. (It would not be amiss to say that *when their claims are equal* fair treatment insists upon seeing people as interchangeable units).

One of the salient elements of fairness is thus that identically situated people should be treated identically. Economists call this the principle of "horizontal equity."[6] But, of course, what is really at issue is neither a principle of justice nor a principle of economic utility but simply one of rationality. For where there is no specifiable difference in condition there is no earthly reason to treat the one case differently from the other. Here the Principle of Sufficient Reason holds sway.

One recent writer tells us that "the principle of fairness . . . [requires] that the benefits to a person from the actions of others are greater than the cost to him of doing his share." The idea is that cooperative and attributive action creates a "bonus" over and above what is produced by the separate activities of the cooperating individuals, and that fairness requires (at least) that everyone should have some share of this resulting benefit. But however plausible this might seem in the abstract as a general rule, it will certainly fail to hold in various sorts of situations. The individual picked by lot to make a sacrifice for the general benefit (the public official designated by lot in ancient Athens, say, or the individual drafted into military service) are not being treated in violation of the principles of fairness. Nor necessarily is the person who loses out when a new highway creates a nuisance for his crops, livestock, and dwelling-place. The "principle of fairness" does not juggle outcomes in the sort of way that this passage contemplates—its prime concern is with process and not product.

But of course people's claims are generally by no means equal. And while distributive procedures that are fair will ipso facto be *equitable*, they need not necessarily be *egalitarian*. For in apportioning allocations to claims, they will perforce treat people very differently when their claims are different. An equality of process need not issue in an equality of product: paying in full is one and the same process, but with larger bills it will yield larger payments. Abstractly considered, fair treatment advantages everyone, on the whole, but it is certainly not true that everyone will benefit from it to the same extent in every instance.

In general, fairness proceeds in abstraction from the personal, idiosyncratic values and preferences of individuals. It is thus not a part of a utilitarian calculus that strives for the greatest good of the greatest number. In particular, honoring the wants and desires of people is something that goes beyond—though not necessarily against!—considerations of mere fairness. Issues of distributive justice, viewed overall, look beyond mere fairness, the equal treatment of parties, to matters of advantage and the general welfare. Advantage differs from fairness. Once a fair distribution has been made, people may well choose to proceed thereafter in making further exchanges in the pursuit of their preferences. Fairness aims at equity, at equitable treatment; it does not try to pre-judge the idiosyncratic desires and preferences of the individuals involved. It is an instrumentality of justice and equity, not of welfare and utility, save insofar as the pursuit of equity at large conduces to the general welfare.

It is one thing to decide what sort of decision is fair and another to implement it in practice. Many writers see the old cake division rule "one cuts, the other chooses" as the very quintessence of the problem of fair division.[7] But this is grossly misleading. There is no "fair division" problem here. The essence of fairness was already settled in advance by the presupposition that the two rivals have equal claims, and whatever "fair division problem" there is here is settled by the ruling that the cake "should be divided equally" between the two (equal) claimants. The only "problem" that remains is the practical one of producing two equal pieces. And this is not an issue of fairness but merely one of partitioning—of finding a means that people are prepared to acknowledge as a practicable procedure for producing an appropriately equal partitioning of something.

Why pursue fairness? Because fairness is an essential component of justice. And homo sapiens is so constituted that unjust treatment offends not just its victims but its bystanders as well. Only in a setting where fairness prevails can we manage to live satisfying lives.

In particular, fair division can avert occasion for rationally warranted envy and dismay at discrimination. But not only can it serve to avoid discontent but wasted effort as well. If we have to meet a joint responsibility (as housemates to do the dishes, as parents to pick Junior up from kindergarten) then by dividing the task between us in a systematic way so that those involved can see it as fair will we avert not only discontent but also the wasted effort required for deciding who does what on a case-by-case basis. Neither justice nor fairness constitutes a be-all of human well-being. But in the final analysis we cannot achieve a satisfactory sort of life without them. And so at the general level of systemic practices there is indeed a connection between fairness and advantage.

4. Fair Division

The paramount consideration for fairness as an aspect of justice is not just how an individual fares in relation to his own claims but how he fares in relation to the rest of the claimants. His very sense of self demands that his just claims be honored at least to the same extent as theirs. Our sense of justice demands that individuals be treated in line with their deserts. Proportioning shares to claims is the only way to achieve his goal.

Moreover, fairness requires deliberation. To count as unqualifiedly fair, a distribution must be made *in order to* realize the demands of fairness. Fair division is a purposive action whose aim is to create a certain end-state, one in which the claims of people are honored. Only persons—conscious deliberate agents—can act fairly. (The differential treatment of people by floods and tornadoes is not unfair but non-fair.) Of course such an agent need not be an individual. Any deliberative corporate agent—a married couple, a corporation, a nation state—is able to act fairly or unfairly.

The concept of justice involves that of proportion: *congruitas ac proportionalitas quaedam*.[8] And in numberless instances that is how it goes in practice. For example, in effecting a settlement in cases of bankruptcy, the standard policy in most modern legal systems is to award shares of the available assets in proportion to the relative size of the claim.

Since justice is a matter of fitness and proportion, it calls for implementing the maxim "according to each what is his own" (*suum cuique tribuere*), and giving everyone "his proper share" goes far back in the history of European thought on the issue.[9] The rule "to each according to his claims"—the "Canon of Claims" as it has been called—is certainly the appropriate principle of distributive justice.[10] Discussions of distributive justice cannot ignore Aristotle's aforementioned emphasis[11] that in a just distribution, shares must be allocated in a way that takes appropriate account of desert or merit (*kata axian*) in terms of the relevant claims of the respective recipients.[12]

The search for a principle of justice is thus brought back to the Roman jurists' dictum that the definitive principle of justice is inherent in the dictum, suum cuique tribuere, "to give each his own," or to Simonides' dictum to *ta opheilomena hekastoi apodidonai dikaion esti,* "to give what is owed to each is just" (see Plato, *Republic* 331d ff.). But what, from the standpoint of distributive justice, can be said to be "his own"? Plainly the answer is "what he deserves," that is, a share ideally equal to his legitimate claims. And here fairness becomes a critical factor.

Most writers on fair division have approached the subject from the direction of economics, decision theory, game theory, and their formalized congeners, basing their calculations on the subjective perspective of the preferences and evaluations of the parties involved. As the authors of an excellent recent book on *Fair Division*[13] put it,

> Our purpose is to find solutions [to decision problems] that reconcile these [conflicting wants,] interests, and principles, insofar as possible in a way that the participants themselves consider satisfactory. Furthermore, we insist that the participants be able to implement their own solution and not have to rely on an outside party, as in the case of arbitration.[14]

This approach differs radically from that of the present book. The problem of fairness, as here conceived, is a matter of doing impartial justice rather than one of pleasing or satisfying the parties involved. Fairness is an instrumentality of the pursuit of justice, not of happiness.

The paramount consideration for fairness as an aspect of justice is not how an individual fares in relation to his own claims but how he fares in relation to the rest of the claimants. His very sense of self demands that his just claims be honored at least to the same extent as theirs. The sense of justice requires that individuals be treated in line with their desert. Proportioning shares to claims is the only way to achieve his goal.

Moreover, fairness requires deliberation. To count as unqualifiedly fair, a distribution must be made *in order to* realize the demands of fairness. Fair division is a purposive action whose aim is to create a certain end-state, one in which the claims of people are honored. Only persons—conscious deliberate agents—can act fairly. Of course such an agent need not be an individual. Any deliberative corporate agent—a married couple, a corporation, a nation-state—is able to act fairly or unfairly.

Can a person be unfair to him or her self? Unquestionably so! One is unfair to oneself if one treats oneself in a way that would be unfair if another person were at issue.

Is life fair? Certainly not literally so—unless one thinks that there is an arranger of human affairs who makes a deliberate distribution, assigning X to be born into a family of wealth and Y to be born into one of poverty quite independently of their deserts. Since fairness requires deliberation, to speak of fairness in relation to one's lot in life is to speak figuratively and anthropomorphically. But of course that figure is true enough as such. It is certainly not the case that life awards people the fate they deserve by proportioning goods and evils to people's appropriate claims.

5. Equality before the State

If a community has a need—or even merely a want, which it sees fit by its duly established decision processes to promote to the status of a need, then its members have the right to demand that *everyone* (myself included!) must do their part, their fair share in meeting that need—like it or not. Doing one's part—bearing one's fair share of the collective burdens of one's society—is certainly one of the key factors in social justice.

However, the claims of individuals upon the state—or the reverse, the claims of the state upon individuals—are not equal. As matters stand in modern advanced societies, the poor and the sick have comparatively greater claims for remediative support, and the state's claims upon the resources of its people fall differently upon the rich and poor in matters of taxation and again upon the young and the old in matters of military service.

"Everyone is equal before the law," says the Universal Declaration of Rights of 1948, reasserting an ideal that has been prominent on the agenda of socio-political thought since the time of the French Revolution. Legal equality can take many forms. It can, for example, operate in matters of voting—"one person, one vote." But it can operate elsewhere as well. The Roman law of persons required unanimity for decisions in matters of guardianship, collective responsibility, and joint property; and public law similarly required unanimity for authorizing interventions by the tribunes of the people. In these matters, even plebeians had the power of negative control—of preventing action.

Equality before the law certainly does not imply *unqualifiedly* equal treatment. It does not require treating literally everyone exactly alike—the perpetrator and the victim, the guilty and innocent. All that equality before the law requires is that (1) people in the same category be treated alike, and (2) that these categories themselves be established in functionally appropriate ways. When sentencing someone for felonious acts, it is in order to distinguish between first-time and repeat offenders, but not so with distinguishing between red-haired offenders and those who are not so. Some differences in condition are claim differentiating and others not.

Traditional conservatism holds that the tendency of humans to act against the interests of others makes it prudent for individuals to accept the restraint of a common political authority that renders them equal before the law. Traditional liberals arrive at the same result as people's shared need for cooperation with others. And idealists argue similarly for the inherently equal worth of humanity. But, of course, all such considerations go no further than to argue for a politico-legal equality quite different from an equality of social or economic condition. That these latter can be validated through considerations of general principle is not only unclear but eminently doubtful because differences in the make-up of people created different demands in point of incentives and motivations.

Even as *equality before the law* is a fundamental principle of justice, so is *equality before the state*. Here again, "equal treatment" certainly does not mean "equal shares" in the goods and bads that the state distributes. The greater burden of military service must be borne by the youthful in contrast to the very young or the very old. A greater amount of taxation will have to be paid by the rich than by the poor. A sensible egalitarianism is emphatically not one of an equality of product (that is, of goods), but one of an equality of process—of equal treatment in relation to claims. But throughout, people in relevantly equivalent conditions will have equal claims on the due process and procedure—and fairness accordingly requires that they be accorded an "equal treatment" not by way of the same treatment but rather by way of treatment in line with the same functionally appropriate principles.

The salient considerations are twofold: (1) that everyone gets treated according to generally understood and accepted rules, and (2) that wherever these rules make for differences, there is a cogent rationale of good reasons for this: if X is to be treated differently from Y, there should be a sound reason of general principle why this should be so, where the principles involved make good sense in terms of efficacy in the functional context at issue.

Of course there may not be detailed precision about this. Generally, there is clearly good reason to defer the age for voting or marrying or driving or military service or entry contracts until the age of adulthood—but whether this is to be seventeen or eighteen or twenty-one can quite legitimately be a matter of local convention. There is a valid rationale of legitimization but it is not something precise. So one cannot complain of unjust treatment in being denied the right to marry which is granted to one's cousin of the same age in a different jurisdiction a few miles away.

Despite the tendency of moral theorists to see the wealth produced in a country as a matter of "social product," the fact of it is that "society" produces no wealth at all. Wealth is produced by individuals—by the entrepreneurs who organize productive effort, the investors who finance it, the workers who give it implementation, and the distributors who make it available to people. It is these wealth-creators who are, in consequence, predominantly situated for establishing claims upon it. Those theorists who worry about "whether people have a fair share of the good things that our society's productivity makes possible" usually forget that such fairness is a matter not of head-count proportionality but of proportionality to claims. And insofar as it is the economic claims of individuals that rest on the extent of their exertions and the fruits of their labors, such contribution-based claims are certainly far from equal. In a world of unequal claims, a rigorously egalitarian state that is committed to an equality of condition is certain to be one that is neither just nor fair.

The idea of *justice*—that people should be treated in line with their appropriate claims—is certainly older and more fundamental than that of *equality*, that people should be treated equally by the society and its laws. In fact, the impetus of modern egalitarianism is not so much towards the positivity that people should be treated equally as towards the negativity that certain sorts of conditions do not make for a disparity of claims that can validate preferential treatment.

The great landmarks of modern egalitarianism illustrate this vividly:

- The French Revolution of 1792 worked to rule out social class (aristocrat/clergy/commoner) as a basis for differential treatment by the law.

- The German Revolution of 1848 worked to rule out economic class (common laborer, bourgeois professional) as a basis of differential treatment.

- The American Civil War of 1865 worked to rule out birth-condition in pursuit of slave or free as a basis for differential treatment by the law.

- The Suffragist Movement of 1905-20 worked to rule out sex as a basis for differential treatment in political matters and its Feminist Movement after World War II worked to rule this out as a basis for differential treatment in economic matters.

All such movements strove to eliminate certain particular, variously targeted factors from qualifying as claim-differentiating. And even such movements as Utopian Socialism has not sought to invalidate claim-differentialism in general. Its precept "From each accordingly to their ability, to each accordingly to their needs" explicitly acknowledges claim differences both on the side of contentions and on the side of benefits. No rational economico-political ideology has ever denied the justice inherent in a principle of differential claims: the argument has only been over what sorts of differences are properly claim-validating.

The history of concern for fairness is thus that of an increasingly ample recognition that where there is equality there must be uniformity of treatment and that equality is ampler than people once thought because over an increasing range of cases there are differences that make no differences—that just do not matter for the ethical issue of how people should be treated. But, of course, once this is said there remain those differences that do matter. However ardently one may espouse the dictum that "all men are created equal" and come into the world with exactly the same status regarding claims, merit, and deserts, there is no gainsaying that this situation is radically altered once men begin to act. Human actions—or at any rate, the great bulk of them—are inherently claim-modifying. No sensible person would want to hold that when the prize is to be awarded, there is no difference in the claims of the winner and the loser of a bet. Few among us would hold that when the payroll is disbursed, the employer should be governed by the rule of equal shares or of "the greatest happiness of the greatest number," indifferent to the question of who are his workmen and who are not. Life is replete with "claim-creating circumstances" typified by the making (and breaking) of promises and contracts. It lies in the nature of things that most distributions are of the functional sort that is unavoidably claim-oriented. The purposive nature of human activity means that no acceptable ethical theory can articulate its principle of choice among alternative distributions of goods and evils in abstraction from a consideration of the legitimate claims of the individuals at issue.

Fairness is no respecter of persons as such, but rather a respecter of their claims. What it calls for is not so much a matter of equality as one of impersonality—of (1) treating everyone by the same rules and principles as everyone else, and (2) making sure that insofar as differently situated people are treated differently by these rules and principles that their differences rest on an adequate rationale of social-benefit considerations. Fairness is thus something quite different from a crude egalitarianism. For fairness is a matter of claim proportionality, and only where people's claims are equal will the demands of fairness and rigorous equality come to coincide.

Procedural equality, treating like cases alike, is an inherent part of practical rationality. For when cases are alike then there is (by hypothesi) no identifiable reason for treating them differently.

When—and insofar as—a social order is populated and operated by irrational beings there is little that we can reasonably do with it. But when it is populated and operated by rational beings, then procedural equality is clearly the most sensible basis for its modus operandi; seeing that rational beings will by virtue of this condition insist upon being treated as such. Accordingly, when we are dealing with rational agents, a social order is more readily instantiated and most stably maintained when its processes are based upon principles of procedural equality. For rational beings will not be content with anything less.

6. Impartiality

The idea of impartiality plays a pivotal role in fairness.[15] And the prime arena for impartiality is the realm of bureaucracy. As Max Weber stressed, bureaucracy "is a key arena for impartiality, seeing that it is marked by the dominance of a sort of formalistic impersonality...[where] the dominant norms are concepts of straightforward duty without regard to personal considerations."[16] Such formalistic impersonality does not amount to crude egalitarianism. It does not treat everyone alike—the school student and the fireman, the corporal and the commanding general.

When they are acting in a public capacity—as military officer, say, or as the captain of a ship—we expect people to treat those within their jurisdiction impartially in a way that we would not expect when dealing with people in a private capacity. And this is, at bottom, a matter of claims. Social realities being as they are, his relations, his neighbors, and his fellow citizens across town all have different sorts of claims on an individual. To treat them interchangeably would be as absurd as treating one's employees and one's customers interchangeably when it comes to setting up the payroll. But when the ship is sinking the random passenger has just as good a claim on the captain's solicitude for her safety as said captain's wife. The conscientious functionary owes impartial treatment to his clients less in virtue of their claims than in virtue of the claims of his office. Impartiality as a cardinal principles of justice. The equality of treatment it requires is entirely dependent upon an equality of claims.

What impartiality demands is not a uniformity of treatment but a uniformity of treatment-governing principles—objective standards of assessment that are applicable to all parties alike. Already Aristotle was at pains to insist that impartial and objective standards are a critical aspect of justice, seeing that its task is to intermediate between the parties and maintain due proportion among them, which clearly requires a common measure.[17]

What is it that makes the unwarrantedly differential treatment of individuals unfair? Again, it is crucially a matter of claims. Consider exclusionary practices. Why is it ethically acceptable to exclude men from a women's basketball team but not ethically acceptable to exclude women from a men's business club? The difference lies entirely on the difference in claims that is grounded in the functional nature of the enterprise. The rationale of a women's sports team is to provide the basis for sporting competitions among women. To allow mixed sex teams unravels the reason for being of the whole venture as an exercise in team sports. On the other hand, the raison d'être of a business club is to provide for social contacts among people who have business dealings with one another. To exclude women is not only unwarranted but is contrary to the very nature of the enterprise.

Impartiality, then, does not require equal treatment as such. Rather—to reemphasize—what it requires is that whenever there is unequal treatment this must have a validating rationale rooted in some inherently appropriate functional aspect of the enterprise at issue. And fairness, correspondingly, consists in conforming distributive practices to impersonal rules of procedure that are justified on the basis of efficacy in serving the legitimate purposes of the human community.

One further important point deserves to be noted. Just as people could speak gramatically before the invention of grammar, so they could display a sense of foul play before the conceptualization of fairness, as such. Fairness as a moral concept is, in a way, a Johnny-come-lately on the stage of ethical desiderata. And it is clear why this should be so. For the idea involved functions at the order of higher-level considerations, and fairness is, as it were, a fourth-level principle. At the base level of concern come actions and behaviors. At the next level come the processes and procedures by which these actions are governed. At the next level of sophistication come the principles and rules that govern those processes and procedures. And only at the next, fourth level, do we arrive at the higher-order principles of uniformity of application with regard to those rules and principles. It is thus only at a rather elevated sophisticated level of thought about matters of moral interaction that the concept of fairness comes into its own as an essential instrumentality of explanation in matters of evaluation and appraisal. While it is generally easy to spot violations of fairness and justice, this is not so with the principles involved—the conceptualization of just what it is about them that marks those violations as improper and reprehensible.

Appendix on Terminology

It is useful to inventory a few terms that will play a more or less technical role in the subsequent discussion of fair distribution.

Dividendum: that which is to be divided.

Bundle: a group of items constituting part of the dividendum.

Claimants: the parties involved in the division on the basis of their claims.

Allocation: either the process of division or the share given to one of the claimants.

Share: the portion of the dividendum received by one of the claimants in the wake of an allocation.

Claim: the share that a claimant ought "by rights" to have.

Entitlement: the share that is appropriate to allocate to an individual in the actually prevailing circumstances.

Note that a dividendum can be either something positive or something negative: it can consist either of goods (positivities) or of bads (negativities). Moreover, the dividendum can be either fixed or variable; in the former case we are bound to have a zero-sum division.

Notes

1. Aristotle, *Nicomochean Ethics*, 1131a30.
2. Broome 1991, p. 199.
3. See H. F. Jolowicz, *Historical Introduction to the Study of Roman Law*, end ed. Cambridge: Cambridge University Press, 1952).
4. See Hart and Honoré 1955. This policy would, however, be foolish if one of the parties could not be identified, for then the only sensible thing to do is to allocate total liability to the known malefactor.
5. A case of this sort is discussed in Broome 1991, p. 194. However, Broome's discussion here does not look beyond the equal-rights situation.
6. The contrast is with "vertical equity" which has to do with identically situated groups. See Atkinson and Stiglitz 1980, pp. 353-55.
7. See Stevataus 1948, Duhms and Spanier 1961, Hart 1985, Brams and Taylor 1996.
8. G. W. Leibniz: *Juris ac aequi elementa*, in *Mitteilungen aus Leibnizens ungedruckten Schriften*, ed. G. Mollat (Leipzig: H. Haessel, 1893), pp. 22 ff.
9. See Plato, *Republic*, 1, 6, 331E and Aristotle, *Nicomachaen Ethics*, V, 5.
10. See Rescher 1966, pp. 81-83.
11. *Nicomachean Ethics* V. 5, 1130b31-33, and V. 6, 1131a20-27. Cf. W. D. Ross, *Aristotle* (5th edn.), pp. 210-11.
12. "It is often held by theologians that in the next world all the accounts will be set straight, that everyone will receive just what he deserves and that therefore there will be 'perfect justice.' Kant, in fact, used this position as an argument for immortality; the moral law requires justice (apportionment of reward to desert), and in this world justice often does not triumph; therefore there must be a life after this one in which it does. As an argument, most philosophers agree that this one is not successful. But at least it is a testimonial to the widespread and deep-seated desire for justice." John Hospers, *Human Conduct*, (New York: Hacourt-Brace World, 1961), pp. 433-34.
13. Brams and Taylor 1996.
14. *Op. cit.*, p. 7
15. For an informative discussion of impartiality see Barry 1995.
16. Max Weber, *Economy and Society* ed. by G. Roth and C. Wittick (Berkeley & Los Angeles: University of California Press, 1988), p. 145. Impartiality knows no distinction of persons. Weber himself to the contrary notwithstanding, it is not (or should not be!) "dehumanized," but it indeed is *depersonalized*. When he comes within the orbit of the law or of the state, it should not matter *who* a person is, all that should matter is *what* he is in terms of the relevant—and to reemphasize, *relevant*—conditions.
17. Aristotle, *Nicomachaean Ethics*, 1131b25-1132a20.

2

Abstract Fairness and Claim Proportionality

(1) Abstract fairness requires that the allocation of shares in proportion to claims must be seen as a cardinal principle of distributive justice. (2) The claim assessment at issue here is a fundamentally objective matter. (3) There are other principles, rival to claim-proportionality, that can (in theory) provide for allocation rules. (4) But in the context of justice none have the distinctive advantages afforded by the claim proportionality at issue with fairness.

1. Strict Fairness

There are many sorts of reasons for giving something to someone: to render them indebted to us, to salve our conscience, to support their efforts because we like them. But fairness only comes into it when they are given something in partial or total satisfaction of a legitimate claim that they have.

According to Webster's *Dictionary*, fairness in dividing goods and bads is a matter of putting personal feelings and concerns aside by avoiding prejudice or favoritism through acting in line with an impartial objective standard of what is just. The range of potential synonyms include: equitable, impartial, even-handed, unbiased, dispassionate. Fairness is thus a matter of treating everyone on the same basis of justifactory appropriateness, irrespective of the agent's predilections or the subject's desires. A fair allocation is impartial and makes sure that everyone gets their due irrespective of how they— or others—may feel about it. A fair distribution accordingly is one that would be made in the circumstances at issue by an objective outsider anxious to avoid any and all plausible charges of partiality.

A formula once offered by Henry Sidgwick has it that justice is the similar and injustice the dissimilar treatment of similars. But such a principle that sees justice as being merely a matter of adherence to the rule, *Treat likes alike*! is clearly inadequate, because it encompasses only a part of the story. After all, a division that is totally inappropriate and unjust can nevertheless manage to treat likes alike. Recognizing this, Sidgwick went on to hold that the "equity principle" under consideration must be supplemented by a "proportionality principle" that the shares of the distribution be proportionate to claims.[1] And indeed abstract fairness—the allocation of shares in proportion with claims—is generally seen as a cardinal principle of distributive justice.

Fairness thus depends critically upon the determination of claims. And one of its cardinal features is an indifference to persons. In particular, whenever there is an equality of entitlement claims, a fair allocation procedure must be indifferent under exchanges of shares among these equity entitled claimants—it must see all such interchanges as equally acceptable. "Treat people whose claims are equal in a strictly equivalent way" is perhaps the most fundamental principle of fairness, and it is of the heart and core of fairness that in the case of equivalent claims the shares of claimants must be of an invariant (uniform) value—unchanged under permutations in these allocations to recipients.

In general, however, the pivot of distributive fairness is that the ratio of share to claim should be uniform for all recipients, so that the relationship:

$$\frac{\text{claim}}{\text{share}} = \text{constant}$$

should obtain throughout the distribution. Fairness, then, is a matter of how people fare in relation to one another in point of the comparative treatment of their claims. We cannot tell if people are being treated fairly either by looking only at what they get as their own share nor yet only by comparing what they get with what others get. Instead, the crucial factor is *what everyone in the group of recipients gets in comparative relation to their just claims*. Strict fairness is a matter of claim proportionality and is thus a matter of equality of a certain sort, namely equal in terms of units of allocation per unit of claims. In a fair distribution every claimant gets the same amount of goods—not absolutely, however, but relative to the magnitude of his claims. Fairness is thus a matter of equalization—not, to be sure, flat out, but in one important respect, that of claim-proportionality.

The claim-proportionate division of a good clearly requires an objective standard for this good's evaluation. But is this not something altogether unavailable? After all, who is to say what those authentic values are in these times when we seem to have lost the area code needed for calling the Recording Angel? Nevertheless, be this as it may, the prospect of getting a *resonable estimate* of authentic values is still with us. For a plausible and reasonable procedure here is to rely on consensus of the best estimates of those disinterested observers who are well-informed about the matters at issue. And barring such an access to value authenticity we may suppose that an impersonal institution such as "the market" will adequately serve the purposes at hand.

Consider an example. A lecturer combines three sites in a single road-trip lecture tour, travelling from home base to institutions in towns G, H, K, and then back. The round-trip air transport fare is $450. If the visits were done in separate trips, the round-trip fare in each case would be: $200 (to G), $300 (to H), and $400 (to K). Accordingly, the breakdown in allocating that overall cost to the three institutions involved ought to be on a ratio 200:300:400, that is 2/9, 3/9, 4/9, or $100, $150, and $200, respectively. So here a fair cost-allocation process—one general to claims established via the cost of detour-free stand-alone visits—will save each of these institutions half of the travel costs when those lectures are given *en tour* rather than individually. And the institutions are treated equally— not in the sense that the cost allocated to each is the same, but rather because the principle on whose basis costs are allocated is uniformly the same, namely the comparative cost of a stand-alone visit.

Suppose that Aunt Agatha dies and leaves three—equally interesting and valuable—family portraits to her two nephews A and B. The fair division would presumably be a 2:1 grouping with random allocation and perhaps some compensation for the "loser." Then Uncle Albert dies leaving three more. Again a random allocation is called for. But these two fair divisions have an even chance of resulting in an overall 4:2 allocation. Had these six portraits been allocated as a group, a 3:3 division would have been the only fair outcome! As this example shows, successively and separately fair divisions need not combine to constitute a concurrently and collectively fair division.

Valid complaint about the justice of a division of goods is possible on two sorts of grounds: overall insufficiency and fairness. A division is *insufficient* when the total it shares out is unable to meet the relevant claims—for example, when someone dies with debts to the tune of $1,000 but an estate of only $500. On the other hand, a division is *unfair* if it treats some claims in a manner disproportionate to the treatment of others. Fairness is thus a matter not of how claimants are treated purely and simply, but of how they are treated in comparison to one another. Fair distributions must therefore be handled holistically, subjecting specific circumstances to general principles.

To be sure, the concept of fairness reaches out beyond the sharing of commodities. The "goods" that are being allocated can be immaterial. Take precedence for example. In seating dignitaries a round table achieves greater fairness because the invidious distinction between "head" and "foot" is abolished. When ambassadors meet with the head of state, it is fairer if the head goes into the chamber where they are waiting rather than having them enter into his presence in an order which puts some ahead of others. Clearly, however, in such matters of precedence and prestige equal claims call for an equalization of *condition* rather than of *goods* received.

2. Two Basic Principles

Fairness as a matter of objective equity in distribution requires looking at an issue objectively and impersonally. Its task is not to anticipate the contingent circumstances or idiosyncratic preferences of the people involved. This sort of thing has to be left to the parties themselves.[2] How people respond subjectively to the fair shares that come their way is their own personal affair. An impartial arbiter concerned to effect a fair distribution need not, and indeed should not be concerned about this.

Accordingly, one of the fundamental principles of fairness is rooted in the injunction: *Dismiss power*! Consider the following situation. Two nephews inherit a field with half good soil and half poor as in no. I of the following series.

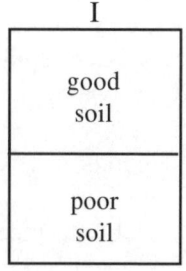 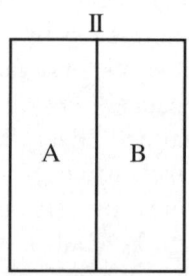 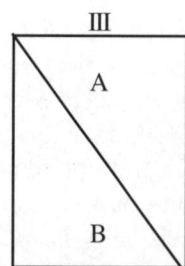

A fair division would proceed as per division No. II where each nephew gets an equivalent half-good, half-bad, 50:50 share. However, it so happens that *A* controls the water supply needed for irrigation and says to *B*: "If you don't accept division No. III, I shall not give you access to water." So *B* confronts a choice between two alternatives:

No. 1:   A quality-balanced half of the field without access to water.

No. 2:   A quality-stinted half of the field but with access to water.

Clearly no. 2 is now *B*'s preferable choice—and obviously *A*'s as well. The result is a consensus with both parties favoring resolution no. 2. What would be wrong with this division? Simply that *A* has used his power posture to effect a distribution that is unfairly favorable to himself. No impartial arbiter would (or should) partition the field as per division III since its two allocations do not divide the good(s) at issue into equivalent shares. A fair resolution must put all considerations of power aside and make an impartial award that dismisses power from consideration. To be sure, after that award is fairly and impartially made, if the parties choose to *renegotiate* it in light of power considerations, then that's their business. But a fair distribution must deliberately discount matters of power. In treating equally qualified claimants alike—as interchangeable units, as it were—fairness assures that power is appropriately sidelined. To reemphasize: it is impartial justice and not political sagacity that is the crux.

A second cardinal principle of fairness is: *Ignore individual preferences*! Ironic though it seems, this is clearly appropriate. Thus, suppose Uncle Theodore dies leaving his collection of four top-grade, three-carat diamonds to his two nieces. As it happens, however, two of them are cut in squares and two in ovals. Niece *A* is especially fond of square-cut diamonds and Niece *B* of oval ones. In allocating two diamonds to each niece, there are thus three possibilities:

1. Each niece gets one of each type.
2. Both square-cuts go to *A*, the others to *B*.
3. Both oval-cuts go to *A*, the others to *B*.

The fair solution is clearly (1) which alone treats the two parties in a strictly equivalent way. To be sure, both nieces would again prefer (2), but that is irrelevant for fairness, which looks to considerations of general principle and leaves idiosyncratic preferences aside. To be sure, after a fair award is made, if the two parties choose to do *horse-trading* in light of their preferences, then that's their business. In approaching the matter of division from the angle of objectivity, fairness renders impartial justice by sidelining personal reactions and preferences.

The answer to the question "What must a fair allocator know about the preferences of the claimants?" is accordingly simply and straightforwardly: Nothing! What he needs to know about is their claims and the basis for them. But that's it. The job of a fair allocation is to level the playing field by making impersonally equitable distributions in a way that assures a procedural equality of process—that meets the demands of impartial justice—that takes the elements of pressure, power, and personal predilection out of it, and proceeds to treat people impersonally rather than as bearers of idiosyncratic wishes, wants, and preferences.

3. On Objectivity: Strict Fairness is not Subjective

Economic theory has long been under the influence of the welfare economists' doctrine that what counts in matters of distribution is the preference ("utility-assessment") of individuals and not simply shares of impersonally valued commodities or money.[3] Accordingly, much of the literature on "fair division" in economics and decision theory has been concerned with preference optimization—the ways and means for effecting distributions that satisfy the desires and preferences of the parties involved. In strict propriety, however, fairness requires a very different approach. Fair shares call for an appropriately claim-proportionalized distribution of objectively defined goods and not of personalized "utility." If two equally entitled claimants are to share four rabbits, two males and two females, fairness demands that each should receive a male-female pair—however ill this might suit the preferences of those involved (let alone the demands of prudence).

On this basis, the common practice of economists of characterizing a distribution among equally deserving recipients as *fair* if it is "envy free" in the sense that none of the recipients involved prefer the share allocated to someone else to that which they themselves receive[4] is gravely deficient. For bringing preferences into it hopelessly psychologizes the issue and relativizes it to individual idiosyncrasies. If *A* out of generosity or self-loathing is happy that his rival *B* shall get the lion's share, that hardly makes the division a fair one. What matters with fairness is clearly not what the claimants prefer with regard to distributions, but rather their inherent preferability—what reasonable people would and should prefer in their place. A division based on preferences conflates justice with paternalistic benevolence.

Fairness in the treatment of claimants does not lie with the subjective satisfaction of the parties involved—any more than justice does. It is something objective and impersonal and calls for an allocation of goods that is strictly impartial from the standpoint of the detached "ideal observer" contemplated by Adam Smith. Such a resolution turns a blind eye to the *wishes and preference* of the parties involved and concerns itself solely with the impartial import of their *justified claims*. The value of what is being divided has to be opposed impersonally—or at least omnipersonally in the aggregate way in which utilities are determined by a "market" that operates on a mass-aggregate basis.

Once personal affinities and valuations are allowed to enter in, we embark on a slippery slope where there is no telling where to stop. After Uncle Robert's death, his umbrella and his cane—items of equal but modest value—are divided between his two nephews by his executor, the former to *A* and the latter to *B*. As it happens, *A*, who was close to the uncle values his item highly while *B* who hardly knew him, sets only a minimal value on his. As a result, *A* fares a great deal better than *B*. Does this unravel the fairness of that initial division? Obviously not. Fairness, as such, goes by objectively and impersonally determinable market values. The idiosyncratic wishes or preferences of the participants—or of the bystanders—have to be left out of it. In matters of justice and fairness personal preferences do not count. After all, they are all too often irrational or unjustifiable. For example, the preferences of those who take pleasure in the sufferings of disabilities of others should clearly count for naught. Rendering people content is not the fair allocator's job. The idiosyncratic preferences and "utilities" of the individuals at issue do not enter into the process of fair division. (If, once a fair division has been effected, they choose to make exchanges or "horse trades" with one another, well and good. But that is something that lies outside the boundaries of fairness.)

Moreover, serious difficulty also undermines the position of those theorists who characterize a fair division among equally entitled claimants as one that is "envy-free" in that no recipient would prefer another's share to his own. After all, people's being envious is simply a matter of psychology and is irrelevant to the issue where what matters is the absence of any rational occasion for envy. Even when the lawn has been divided into perfectly equal parts between two claimants each may well stand gazing enviously over the fence at the other's half because "the grass is always greener on the other side." But of course what really matters is not the absence of envy but the absence of any valid occasion for it. The crux of fairness is equality of treatment on the basis of general principles that take appropriate account of valid claims. Unquestionably, the issue of preference-accommodation represents an important and interesting topic. But it is of problematic weight in matters of distributive justice and certainly does not address the matter of fairness as properly understood. The edifice of justice cannot be built up on the shifting sands of people's idiosyncratic attachments.

4. Fairness and Procedural Appropriateness

"Ensure that in the distribution shares are proportional to claims" is the governing principle of fairness. Fairness, accordingly, has two principal components:

1. Adequacy of result—i.e., the claim-proportionate of shares.

2. Appropriateness of process—i.e., the impartiality and even-handedness of the allocation procedure by which this result is achieved.

Irrespective of results, there is no fairness in the absence of an equitable proceeding under the aegis of uniformly applied general principles. Thus, if two differentially noted items (one worth $10 and one $100) are to be divided between two differentially entitled claimants (one due $10 and the other $100) the interests of fairness have not been served by a coin toss which just happens to give the right result.

It would be very nice if we could separate process from product here and speak separately of fair shares and the fairness of the distribution process by which they are arrived at. Unfortunately, that just does not work—or, at any rate, not in general—because of the *interaction* between process and product here. Three marbles are to be divided between two boys whose claims are equal. For starters each gets one marble. Fine! But what about the odd one, is it to go to Bob or to Tom? They'll simply have to toss for it. Let it be so, then let's say that Tom wins. Then the result is: two for Tom, one for Bob. Is that distribution fair? Well...yes and no. Given the situation as described, this result is perfectly fair—the two lads had equal chances for that second marble. But had that very selfsame distribution been arrived at differently—say by an allocator who simply favored Tom—then it would be eminently unfair. The lesson is clear: we cannot in general separate fairness of result from fairness of process. Only when it has been fairly arrived at can that fair result be characterized as such.

Sometimes process even takes priority over product in matters of fairness. Suppose a farmer dies with a will specifying that his two sons are each to have one of his two statutorily indivisible fields, without specifying which field goes to which son. And suppose further that these fields differ in productivity in that one is substantially more fertile than the other. We face here a situation of forced choice between two alternatives:

	Distribution No. 1	*Distribution No 2*
Son A	Fertile field	Infertile field
Son B	Infertile field	Fertile field

Note that, by hypothesis, the option of a fair outcome is simply not directly available here. Fairness must now be realized not at the level of the distribution itself but only at the level of the distribution process—presumably one random choice.

The fair allocation of a given dividendum must be based upon claims and claims alone. It is thus crucial to fairness in distribution that insofar as there is a difference in outcome no other factor save differences in claims come into its determination. Here precisely is why random selection is such a crucial factor for fairness, for the very randomness at work precludes the operation of any inappropriate reasons for the outcomes arrived at. The case of a shortage of transplantation organs such as kidneys affords an example. When there are fewer organs than can meet the needs of a group of equally eligible patients, a random selection or process along the lines of a lottery is clearly the only fair way to proceed. Not only does it give all claimants an equal chance, but merit lies in the very absence here of any cogent reason why one particular outcome is arrived at rather than another.[5]

5. Allocating Fair Shares

Discussions of distributive justice would be well advised to speak of its mission in terms of *allocating* goods rather than *dividing* them. For not only are many sorts of goods indivisible but some do not actually need to be divided because they are fissionable: they simply multiply to whatever extent is necessary and appropriate to the occasion. Thus in the case of a co-discovery by two persons in science or in exploration, both get full credit as discoverers. If a monetary prize is involved they may have to share it (money is not fissionable). But with credit it is otherwise. Both co-discoverers deserve full credit—both count as discoverers: they need not divide the honor of the thing and count simply as half-discoverers. If medals are to be awarded they will each get one. And the same is true on the negative side. If two parties collaborate in the crime then both will count as murderers, assassins, fraudsters: neither the blame nor the penalty gets divided between them.

A good may be *homogeneously divisible* into smaller awards (like money, or precious metals, for example). Failing that, it may be *partitionable* and allow of being broken into component parts or bundles of separable constituents (like a collection of books or stamps or artwork). And failing that, it may allow of plausible *timesharing* like a vacation cabin or a portrait of the family patriarch and unlike a plane ticket or an aristocratic title. If all of these fail and we have a good that is indivisible, unpartitionable, and unshareable, then such a good may be characterized as *atomic*, it is something that cannot be divided up in any way, manner, or shape. Often, goods that are not actually atomic are treated as such for practical purposes because the parties involved are simply not prepared either to partition or to share them. Such goods, too, are commonly characterized simply as *indivisible*.

When it comes to allocating fair shares, the nature of the good at issue is accordingly going to play a crucial role, one that is determinative for the question of the appropriate modus operandi. And in matters of distributive justice there is a distinctive pecking order of priority for proceeding with allocations:

1. *Division.* Insofar as possible, divide the goods to be allocated themselves—and thus always do so when dealing with a divisible and homogenous commodity.

2. *Partition.* When the goods to be allocated are differentiated (nonhomogeneous) then group them insofar as possible into bundles of equivalent value and divide such bundles among the claimants. Thereupon one should, insofar as possible, provide for compensating adjustments (e.g., side-payments) to provide compensation where the bundlings are not value-equivalent.

3. *Timesharing.* When goods are neither homogeneously divisible nor such that they can be grouped into a suitable plurality of value-equivalent bundles, then share out access time among the claimants (i.e., have them "take turns") insofar as this is practicable.

4. *Monetization.* When all of the above fail, then do what can be done to realize the value of those goods and divide their monetary value.

5. *Randomizing.* When all of the above fail then make a distribution by lottery via a suitably randomized distribution (possibly with side payments to proportionalize the value of the shares).

There is a definite priority ordering here that starts out from the ideal of actual division, and then endeavors to keep as close to this ideal as the circumstances of the case make possible. However, what forces one to move down that priority list is the impossibility or impracticality of the prior procedures. Consider an example: Smith dies leaving the whole of his estate to his two daughters. Its only item of value is a rare old master painting. It makes no sense to cut it in two—so (1) is out. There is only one item to be distributed—so (2) is out. Thus (3) is the first seemingly viable option. But if this is impracticable (say because the painting is too large to fit into the daughters' houses or because they cannot afford the cost of insuring the painting and shipping it back and forth), then it is (4) that provides the path to fairness.

It needs to be emphasized that it is inappropriate—and indeed unfair and unreasonable—to proceed out of sequence here. Suppose that Aunt Harriet's will specifies that her jewels should go to her two nieces, Jane and Mary. To save himself the trouble of partitioning them, the executor simply makes the nieces draw straws. Thus in the end all goes to Mary and nothing to Jane. But it is, of course, unjust and unfair that one of the claimants should go totally empty handed in these circumstances even though the two of them had an equal chance. That supposedly fair distribution clearly does not adequately honor claims. And its flaw lies in violating that prioritization of process at issue with fairness.

Achieving fairness in particular situations may require a rather sophisticated division process. For example, the traditional cake-division principle, "One cuts, the other chooses" is not really fair—the chooser is bound to come out ahead—to be sure by a quantity that the cutter can control down to rather minute proportions. Proceeding fairly here would require that the relevant roles—cutter and chooser—be determined randomly, say by tossing a coin.

Fairness, it must be reemphasized, is not just a matter of product but of process. It is not just a matter of value received but depends critically upon the ways and means by which that result is effected. A particular allocation process may be fair in some circumstances but not in others. In the case of theater seats, for example, or a department store sale, "first come, first serve" is neither unreasonable nor unfair. But in that of a bankruptcy settlement or a bank collapse it would clearly not be so because "insiders"—and those close to them—would have an unmerited advantage.

Figuring out effective procedures for partitioning differently structured sorts of complex objects in line with specified proportions is a problem that has preoccupied mathematical economists for several decades now.[6] But these ramifications need not concern us here. For while this sort of thing has considerable formalistic interest and poses intriguing theoretical challenge, these intricacies do not affect the issues of principle that govern the ethical aspects of the matter where issues of distributive justice are concerned.

6. Randomness: A Last Resort

Theorists who have a special fondness for lotteries and similar modes of random allocation have had a good deal of difficulty with the idea of satisfaction of claims, rights, and deserts. Indeed, one of them is driven to the rather desperate expedient of holding "that the concept of desert is incoherent and, philosophically speaking, unfounded."[7] But only isolation in an ivory tower can protect such a theorist from an awkward encounter with sociopaths, employees, and war heroes—people whose placement in point of claims is all too obviously different from that of others. It is clear that such randomness vehicles as lotteries have an important role in matters of distributive justice. But it is no less clear that this place will have to be restricted in its scope and its range.

As the preceding deliberations indicate, random allocation of a dividendum to just one of the claimants is a measure of last resort. It is appropriate only when two conditions are met:

1. There must be no viable alternative. The case must be such that physical division, timesharing, sell-and-divide, etc. are all inappropriate.

2. Insofar as possible, appropriate measures must be taken to see to it that all of the nonrecipients are duly compensated in line with their respective claims; they are entitled to compensation, seeing that they do not share in the dividendum, as such, they are entitled to share in its value.

There are, however, two exceptions to clause 2, as follows:

i. The omission of compensation is in order when the allocation at issue relates to the starting-position (the "opening move," so to speak) of a take-turns process. (Serving first at tennis, for example, or making the opening move at chess.)

ii. The omission of compensation is in order in extreme situation where, in effect, those who lose out elude the prospect of compensation because they die. (Randomly selecting the victim for cannibalism or for "throwing to the wolves" in extreme circumstances.)

In the realm of first and last steps, so to speak, questions of compensation do not arise. As noted above, a premature leap ahead to a probabilistic allocation is in fact a departure from the demands of fairness. Not to give the better-than-average worker a bigger-than-average raise but only a bigger-than-average *chance* of getting it in a lottery is simply unfair. Nor in settling and estate with some valuable jewels being divided between two equally entitled heirs would it count as fair to proceed by a lottery that gives each a 50:50 chance at a winner-take-all allocation. Randomness must take its due place at the end of the line. It should come into operation only when actual division, equivalency-bundling, timesharing, and market-sell-off are inapplicable or impracticable.[8] Such cases of course exist, as various readily available examples indicate.

Case 1. A, *B*, and *C* have accidentally ingested a fatal poison. However, we have two grams of an antidote that is invariably effective at a 1-gram dose and invariably ineffective at a lesser dose. Q: Who is to get what, seeing that it is clearly pointless to give each party two-thirds of a gram? Regrettable though this may be, the only plausible proceeding is that two of the three, chosen randomly, should get a 1-gram dose. Here allocating claim-proportionate shares is useless since this abandons the crucial feature of survivable conduciveness. So, division being inappropriate, we proceed to randomness. The actual claim of each party is not to two-thirds of a gram but to a survival-adequate amount. Since there are only two of these for the three parties, the unfortunate nonrecipient must be selected randomly.

Case 2. A, B, and C are adrift in a lifeboat in the rainfree latitudes of a vast ocean. They have a 6-gallon supply of water. Who gets what? The answer here is that it must be divided equally among them (presumably via equally modest rations). But why not allocate a larger portion to just two, chosen randomly as in the preceding antidote case? Because equal shares are now pointful, seeing that in *these* circumstances they have a survival promoting-potential. So we don't get past equal shares to randomness in that procedural hierarchy. The point is that resort to the concept of "fairness of opportunity" is a *faute de mieux* procedure, a Plan B counsel of last resort, as it were that, that should come into operation only when a direct allocation of shares to claims is infeasible.

One fairness theorist writes that, with lotteries, having a claim-proportionate chance "is a sort of surrogate satisfaction of the claim."[9] But what is at issue with randomness in distribution is not a matter of a make-do surrogate satisfaction of a claim but rather a response to the circumstance that actual claim-satisfaction is simply impracticable.

7. Egalitarian Justifications of Proportionality in Distribution

Even where different people have different claims that require a difference in response, a claim-proportionate division nevertheless qualifies as a mode of evenhandedness. Suppose, for example, that a shortfall is to be allocated among competing estate only suffices to pay half the decedent's debts). And let us suppose that—as seems to be plausible—a claimant is chagrined ("feels his loss") to a degree that varies inversely with the percentage recovered. (That is, 10 percent recipients feel twice as put upon as those who receive 20 percent of what they can properly claim.) It is then readily seen that to equalize chagrin we must distribute the assets involved on a claim-proportionate basis.

Again, let us suppose that an individual's dismay and outrage in the case of a shortfall stands in proportion to how his own shortfall measures up against his assigned share:

$$\text{Disappointment} \approx \frac{\text{shortfall}}{\text{share}} = \frac{\text{claim} - \text{share}}{\text{share}} = \frac{\text{claim}}{\text{share}} - 1$$

In a fair division shares are proportional to claims and in consequence of this we have: $\frac{\text{claim}}{\text{share}} = \text{constant}$

This means that a fair, claim-proportionate division—and this only—will occasion uniformly equal dismay and disappointment among claimants in the case of a shortfall. So here again fairness is a means to equity.

A good case can thus be made for holding that an egalitarian management of chagrin and dismay requires claim-proportionate distribution, so that there is, in fact, a close interlinkage between fairness and an egalitarianism of sorts. Accordingly, the gulf between egalitarian and proportionate distribution is not as wide as it might appear. For egalitarian distribution of psychic goods would, under plausible conditions, be equivalent to a claim-proportional division of material goods. And so insofar as one is prepared to accept the idea that fair distributions should aim at equality with respect to psychic goods, one is naturally led to endorsing the principle of claim-correlative distributions. Fairness and equality of treatment will go hand-in-hand here.

8. Negativities

Fairness is not, of course, a matter of the equitable distribution of positive goods alone but also of negative "goods"—that is, of "bads." For example, consider three apartment sharers who must perform certain chores along the lines of shopping, taking out the garbage, etc.[10] Perhaps the most unproblematically fair way of handling this over the long term is by a scheme of rotation, of taking turns at these various chores. But what if the time period is too short to make this practicable?

One way of proceeding will set out from the market value of the tasks involved, which in this case may be supposed to be as follows:

Chore	Market Price (of hiring someone to do the chore)
shopping	$20
cooking	$60
dishwashing	$45
cleaning	$40
garbage disposal	$15

Since the cost of getting a task done may be taken to reflect the onus it involves, the plausibly fair thing to do is to bundle the tasks into equi-costly groups and allocate them randomly to the parties involved. The groups would be something along the lines of:

- shopping and cleaning
- cooking
- dishwashing and garbage disposal

Such a process of random equal-onus allocation minimizes the scope for justifiable complaints about fairness.

9. Different Sorts of Claims

But if fairness calls for claim proportionality, then what happens when there are several ways of establishing claims, each of them inherently reasonable?

Consider an example. A country with a population of 40 million inhabitants is composed of ten regions, six of them small, with only one million inhabitants the other four substantially larger. By the country's constitution, the National Assembly is to have 500 members, elected on a regional basis. How many representatives should each of those four small regions have if the fairness principle of "one person, one vote" is to obtain?

Note that each small region has one-fortieth of the population, so that its representation should be one-fortieth of the National Assembly membership or 12.5 members. Half members are, of course, difficult to come by. One must either round down to 12 or up to 13. If the former is done, then those six small regions will have a total of 72 members so that small-regions-in-general will have 14.4 percent of the Assembly membership. If the latter is done, those six small regions will have a total of 78 members and thus those small-regions-in-general will have 15.6 percent of the Assembly membership.

Thus in the former case, the ratio of small to large region representatives will be 72:428 = 16.8, while in the latter case the ratio of small to large region representatives will be 78:422 = 18.5. But, of course, the actual population of those six small regions is six out of forty million and so by rights the ratio of small-to-large region representatives should stand at an intermediate 17.6. Whichever way we turn, we are bound to encounter the complaint that those small regions are either under- or overrepresented in relation to their larger compeers.[11]

To achieve fairness in the small vs. large regional representation we would have to resort to randomness in our allocation process. In the endeavor to proceed reasonably here, we could first allocate to those small regions 12 members each and then by a random process pick (3) additional at-large small regional representatives. And even this process would not work if (unlike the present case) the count of those "missing" representatives did not work out to an even number.

And so what we have here is a two-sided situation—conflict between two rival standards of equality: voter-representation equality vs. region-representation equality. In such a case fairness cannot speak with an undivided mind.

Consider another example. Two communities are deliberating about starting up a common 911 emergency call system. Town 1 can develop a facility of its own for $5 million, town 2 can do so for $4 million. The creation of a common facility would cost $7 million. By cooperation, the towns could thus save $2 million. How should they divide the costs?

Several sensible-looking approaches come to mind.

Approach No. 1 (Share savings equally). The towns save $2 million, which they should divide equally because "each counts for one." So the cost for town 1 should be $6 - 1 = 5$ million while that of No. 2 should be $3 - 1 = 2$ million.

Approach No. 2 (share costs proportionality). The system costs for the towns stand in the ratio 6:4. So Town 1 should bear 60 percent of the costs or 4.2 million while Town two should bear 40 percent of the costs or 2.8 million. (Note: Sharing *savings* proportionally comes to the same as sharing *costs* proportionally.)

And there is also a plausible third prospect. The two previously indicated approaches are, to all visible intents and purposes, equimeritorious. We might as well split the difference and take the average: Thus 1 should contribute 4.6 million and town 2, 2.4 million. (Somewhat ironically what we have here is a fair-equiproportionate division between two equiplausible approaches to fairness.)

The proportionality measure of fairness is often tricky to implement because the question *proportion-of-what?* is always going to arise in regard to the claims at issue. Thus in the preceding example there are also other plausible ways of establishing claims upon those savings: are those savings to be shared per town, per initial dollar cost, per capita, per dollar tax intake, etc? We arrive at various alternatives:

1. equal savings (per town) [share savings equally]

2. cost-proportionate savings [allocate saving cost proportionately; equalize savings per initial dollar cost]

3. equal savings per capita [equalize savings per capita]

4. equal savings per tax dollar intake [equalize savings per unit income]

To speak meaningfully of "equal savings" one must resolve the issue of savings being equal *per what*? What is the unit on which claims are to be based? Whose claims are at issue: the town, the individual person, the taxpayer dollar, etc.? In such cases, there will be no uniquely cogent basis for determining claims. (As per the earlier suggestion, it might well be the best one can do to survey the whole spectrum of "plausibly fair" solutions and then average out.)

Fairness in the sense of claim-proportionality is critically dependent upon the nature and variety of the relevant claims. And thus when there are several distinct bases for such claims, fairness cannot speak with an undivided mind. Here a charge of unfairness cannot be sustained if it should eventuate that the ideal is unattainable in some respect or other. And so the lesson emerges that where there are different bases for claims we may not be able to achieve fairness in every direction at once. It may again transpire that the best one can do is to "average things out" by letting those different claim-bases come into operation in accordance with their respective weights. In such cases we have to be fair about fairness itself.

Even when people are funneled into the meat grinder of war by way of involuntary military service, justice requires neither an equality of outcome nor even an equality of risk. But what it does require is a uniform application of situation-justifiable rules—uniform not in that individuals are treated exactly alike (the male and the female, the young and the old, the healthy and the sickly). But the rules and procedures by which people are treated must both be appropriate in themselves and also be uniform for all, even though their implimentation does not treat all uniformly.

Strongly normative concepts like fairness, justice, and even rationality resist being captured by any compact synoptic formulation or represented by any single uniformly constructed model, because it lies in the nature of things that so extensive a concept has to accommodate itself to a great variety of particular situations so that a "one pattern fits all" is not a workable prospect.[12]

Notes

1. Sidgwick 1907, p. 279.
2. Fairness is by its nature a matter of distributing goods in the light of their objective and impersonally determinate value. Insofar as the economists' "utility" is something that depends on personal preferences, fairness does not concern itself with utility. For fairness is a matter of distribution and if where there is no such thing as a determinate and impersonal utility, then utility is not something we can distribute. We can at most distribute goods that have a (differential) utility for different individuals. And if (or rather since) the economists' utility is not interpersonally impossible such utility is something we cannot distribute in equal (or otherwise proportionate) ways. All we can do is to try to satisfy the recipients, and this preference-oriented perspective is exactly how the economists look at it. But justice and fairness call for something else.
3. In economics this is plausible because only where we value things differently—only if I prize your apples more than my oranges and you do the reverse—will we make an exchange.
4. See, for example, Sen 1970. This approach goes back at least to Foley 1967. See also Feldman and Kerman 1974, Varien 1974, Thomson and Varian 1985, Baumol 1986, and Roemer, 1994.
5. See Nicholas Rescher, "The Allocation of Extra Medical Lifesaving Therapy," *Ethics*, vol. 79 (1969), pp. 173-86.
6. One such mathematically sophisticated problem, for example, is that of devising a general process for dividing a cake into n pieces in such a way that assures each recipient of equal shares of icing and of cake. See Hart 1985, Hill 2000.
7. B. Goodman 1992, p. 64.
8. Goodman, 1992 is an informative discussion of relevant issue which rightly stresses the inherent even-handedness of lotteries as a distributive process. It does not, however, sufficiently recognize their last-resort aspect as an instrumentality of distributive justice.
9. Broome 1991, p. 196.
10. For a discussion of this example from a point of view variant from that of the subsequent discussion see Brams and Taylor 1996, p. 49.
11. The situation envisioned here actually realized in the struggle between the Jeffersonian Republicans and the Hamiltonian Federalists in the founding era of the American republic. For details see Chapter 3, "The Methods of Jefferson and Hamilton" in Balinsby and Young, 1982, pp. 10-48.
12. See Rescher 1994 and compare Wolff 1998.

3

The Liabilities and Assets of Fairness

(1) Fairness is not necessarily popular—a fair resolution need not win out in a majority vote. (2) Moreover, there are various distributive desiderata that fairness lacks. (3) And allocation principles distinct from fairness can have some desirable features. (4) However, certain criticisms of fairness are not appropriate. For example, the problem of indivisible goods need not defeat fairness. (5) Nor is it correct to object that fairness is unachievable with shortfalls in an economy of scarcity.

1. Fairness Does not Seek Popularity nor Honor Power

Impartial justice and fairness are not by nature things that are going to please people generally and conduce to the happiness of all or most. Being treated fairly is less likely to please people than acting in ways that make them feel favored. But no matter. Justice and fairness are important sociopolitical virtues in their own right. Like ideal judges, fair allocators should render impartial justice: they are not populist politicians who see their task as gaining approval by promoting the general happiness. Fairness—like justice—is an austere virtue that is not necessarily popular.

In the real world, a majority of the recipients of a distribution may well gain an advantage from unfairness—simply by dividing the shortfall of the disadvantaged among themselves. And power can also countervail against fairness. As Pascal observed: "Why do we follow the majority? Because it is more right? No! Because it has more power" (*Pensées*, V, 301). The fact of it is that fair division is a *normative* concept. When a division is fair it leaves the parties involved with the least occasion for justified complaint that justice has not been done. It need not, however, be a division that maximizes contentment (or minimizes discontent) within the group concerned, seeing that many might profit by shortchanging a few. Nor does fairness respect power, seeing that, in practice, the sort of power plays represented by elections or coalitions can readily lead to outcomes that favor unfair distributions.

Fairness, to reemphasize, requires commitment to what is impersonal and impartial. And this is by no means to its discredit. After all, here, as elsewhere, there is no guarantee that justice will emerge from the natural interactions among self-interested people. In various circumstances many or most people may prefer to depart from strict fairness. (Of course, this does not—should not constitute an argument that countervails against the claims of fairness.) Let us examine these issues more closely.

2. Distributive Desiderata

Deliberations regarding distributive justice are, like all others, subject to the fundamental general principle that the answer will depend on just exactly what the question is. Confronted with a division situation we can ask such questions as:

- What allocation will the parties involved arrive at through a democratic (majority rules) vote?
- What allocation would the parties involved arrive at in a negotiation?
- What allocation would a benevolent outsider select as being in the best interests of the parties?
- What allocation would an impartial outsider select when proceeding in an impersonal way that treats all parties in the light of their valid claims, ignores both the power relationships and the idiosyncratic preferences of those parties.

We here arrive at four sorts of divisions, the *democratic*, the *negotiative*, the *benevolent,* and the *fair* respectively. It is readily seen that all of these pose different issues that call for different sorts of implementation.

Let us begin with an example. Suppose that an estate of $300 is to be settled in the face of an obligation to three debtors who are due $100, $200, and $300 respectively. Then the fair (claim-proportionate) settlement of 50, 100, 150 respectively will not, in all likelihood, transpose prevail in a democratic vote among the alternatives. After all, the allocation 100, 200, 0 is a more likely result, with the two fully satisfied claimants simply outvoting their short-changed compeer. But, of course, such majoritarian endorsement will not create fairness.

But now suppose that the middle claimant is in a power position to block any settlement whatever. Then he is liable to say to the others, "You better let me have more than my merely 'fair share' of $100, since if you don't concede me a premium then I'll let you two go empty handed 'til the cows come home." In sum, if one party has a power advantage, then he is liable to exploit this to his own benefit in the process of negotiation. This may actually engender an agreement but it is something quite different from fairness. Fairness roots in the validity of claims: it does not—should not—reflect disparities in bargaining power.

Again, suppose that three bicycle wheels and one bicycle chassis are to be divided between two (equally entitled) recipients. A fair distributor is liable to group them in the bundles $c + w$ and $w + w$, followed by a random allocation of the bundles—leaving it up to the parties concerned to strike a bargain that would result in the transfer of the chassis or of the wheel. On the other hand, a benevolent outsider would presumably bundle them as $c + w + w$ and w, now proceeding with a random allocation. After all, a bicycle that has only one wheel is quite useless. Thus fairness is not the same as economic efficiency.

Against this background, consider the array of distributional virtues inventoried in display 1. Note here that a (perfectly) just distribution must be fair, but not conversely. Moreover, while distributive maximality is something objective, all the other features of the second category hinge on the subjective—and potentially irrational—preferences and evaluation of individuals. We shall see below that an envy-free distribution need not be universally popular (nor the reverse!), and that subjectively equitable distribution need not be benevolently optimal or the reverse. However, one conclusion stands out regarding the entries of display 1. Many of them move off in directions very different from the fairness at issue with distributive justice. Maximality and negotiative acceptability bears on the aspect of economic productivity (or "efficiency"); benevolence on that of subjective satisfactions; popularity bears on the sociopsychological dimension. Unlike the entries at the top of the display, none of these have an intimate bearing upon justice itself. They are in this regard very different from fairness as properly understood.

Display 1
Distributive Desiderata

A DISTRIBUTION IS	IF EVERYONE INVOLVED GETS A SHARE OF THE GOOD/BAD BEING DISTRIBUTED THAT IS
(perfectly) just	exactly what meets their (legitimate) claims
fair	proportionate to their claims
supra-fair	sometimes more but never less than their fair share
subjectively equitable	of a self-appraised (subjective) value that is claim-proportionate

A DISTRIBUTION IS	IF IT IS
maximal	so adjusted that the overall distribution is maximized
benevolently optimal	both subjectively equitable and maximal
universally popular	preferred to the alternatives by all parties involved
democratically popular	preferred by the greatest achievable majority of the parties involved
envy-free	such that no recipient would prefer someone else's share to his own
negotiative	such that this distribution would emerge from a negotiation that reflects the preferences (subjective valuations) and the power position of the parties concerned.

Abstractly speaking, it seems reasonable enough to see popularity, benevolence, etc. as representing various virtues (positive assets) for distribution procedures. They do, however, differ from fairness and from one another, and they are not as closely interconnected as one might think. In this regard, the following points deserve particular note.

1. A totally just procedure must indeed be fair, but the reverse need not be so. For in situations of scarcity a fair distribution may come up short in point of claim satisfaction.

2. A fair division need not be democratically popular. A majority of claimants may well favor an unfair division that works in their favor.

3. A fair division need not be subjectively egalitarian because the subjective evaluations of individuals may well be out of line with objective value.

4. Envy-freedom differs from fairness and really does not mean all that much—particularly in cases where people's evaluations are unreasonable.

5. A maximal distribution may well be neither fair nor popular, since that large amount being distributed may well not be shared out justly.

As such considerations show, fairness is a particular sort of distributive virtue with characteristic assets and liabilities of its own.

Point 4 deserves special comment. The aim of mainstream contemporary approaches to fairness is—as one widely cited book on fair division puts it—to persist "in elevating the property of 'envy freeness,' and procedures that generate envy-free allocations, to a central place in the study of fair division."[1] But this is very questionable. For one thing, individuals may have unreasonable wishes and expectations, and thus be envious where this is entirely unreasonable. Moreover, being envy-free is something that has significance only in the special case of altogether equal claims. For consider: a decedent leaves an estate of $600 but owes each of two creditors $300 and a third $600. A fair division calls for giving the first two creditors 150 and the third one 300. No doubt the first two will both envy the third—after all he receives an amount they see as their own due, whereas they receive only half as much. If the estate were divided 300, 300, 0 not only would most claimants have their claims satisfied, but there would be only one who has occasion to envy the shares received by the rest. Nevertheless, such a division is profoundly unfair.

3. A Variety of Allocation Principles

In theory, to be sure, other principles of allocation different from strict fairness are also possible, and some of them seem to have appeal and merit. Three particularly plausible candidates are:

Equal shares: making an equal division among the claimants, irrespective of the magnitude of their claims.

Default minimization: satisfying the greatest number of claims that one can.

Larger-claim precedence: giving greater claims precedence over smaller ones insofar as is practicable.

A schematic example will help to illustrate how these principles function in practice: Suppose that a debtor expires leaving an estate of 100 units and five creditors (A – E) who are owed 20, 20, 20, 40, 100 respectively. The principles at issue would divide the estate in the manner depicted in Display 2.

Display 2
A Hypothetical Illustration

	A	B	C	D	E
Proportionality:	10	10	10	20	50
Equality:	20	20	20	20	20
Default Minimization:	20	20	20	40	0
Larger-claim Precedence:	0	0	0	0	100

By claim proportionality, the creditors' shares comes to 10 percent for each for A, B, C, 20 percent to D, and the remaining 50 percent to E. By equality all claimants get equal shares with each getting 1/5 of that $100. By default minimization A, B, C, and D have their debts settled in full, while E is out of luck. (Observe that a majority vote would presumably endorse this alternative, even though this policy simply stiffs the largest claimants.) By contrast, large-claim predominance gives the major claimant(s) the most-favored treatment, so that in the present case E is the winner who takes all.[2]

Those various procedures yield different results—most of them unfair. An egalitarian will opt for equality. A utilitarian ("the greatest good of the greatest number") would thereby presumably favor default minimization so as to maximize the honoring of claims, and a Rawlsian moralist ("favor the least advantaged") would presumably do the same. By contrast, a ruthless capitalist might well favor the principle of large-claim predominance. However, someone committed to fairness will reject all of these approaches and deploy the principle of claim-proportionality in the interests of optimally accommodating the demands of justice.

On the surface of it, the preceding principles are all formulated in general terms, without prejudicial favor to particular individuals. But whether a given principle provides for a sufficiently impersonal approach is nevertheless open to discussion. Obviously the rule of equality ("All claimants are to get equal shares") meets this requirement. But the rule of large-claim priority ("Meet larger claims in full before turning to smaller ones") does not.

Still, all of those different principles of division seem to have some plausibility. Why should it be that fairness takes priority?

One salient advantage of claim-proportionality fairness is that the fusion of a claimant group's members into collective constituents or this disaggregation into separate units leaves intact the size of the shares available to such units. And since shares are thus invariant under recombinations, the prospect of power plays through threats of alliances or defections is annihilated.

But, of course, the main asset of fairness—of principled equity—is that it alone is proof against charges of the irrationality of treating claimants differently when there is no claim-relevant reason for doing so. The crucial point is that fairness is a demand of reason in the context of distributive justice.

4. Indivisible Goods Need not Defeat Fairness

The ensuing discussion will investigate the credentials of abstract fairness—that is, claim proportionality—to serve as a salient operative principle of just allocation. En route, we must come to grips with the circumstance that various obstacles seem to lie in the way of fairness as a practicable goal, specifically in such matters as:

- allocations of indivisible goods
- allocations of shares in conditions of insufficiency or of superabundance
- allocations of intellectual credit in relation to discoveries
- allocations of legal penalties to accessories in crimes

All of these seeming exceptions to the practicability of fairness need to be examined in detail. And it will emerge that, seeming difficulties notwithstanding, the principle of claim proportionatily can virtually always be sustained.

Let us begin with the first item on the list—the problem of dividing indivisible goods. Clearly, many sorts of goods are unavoidably such that it makes no sense for them to be split into parts—rare paintings or coins for example. But as we have seen, there are—fortunately—fair alternatives to a *physical* division—timesharing for example. The rival claimants to a throne need not fight for it: in theory they could take turns year by year. And even if an asset itself cannot be divided, it can often be sold and its market value then divided. In such oblique ways, then, the element of fairness (and thus of justice) can be introduced even into situations in which straightforwardly fair distributions by the physical division of goods—the ideal of distributive justice—lies outside the range of realizable practicality. But are such detours always available?

5. Fairness Can Accommodate Shortfalls and Windfalls

Some distributive-justice theorists think that claims-proportionate fairness is problematic or even inappropriate in situations of deficit and excess—of shortfalls and windfalls—and that these cases call for special and extraordinary measures. With respect to the former, for example, they consider such variant distribution rules as: that of Shortfall Minimization: "Minimize the maximum shortfall for the individual claimants." However, the fact of it is that even with shortfalls we should, in general, proceed by fair shares. For fair division alone minimizes the proportionate extent to which any claimant is penalized in a shortfall situation. Thus consider the situation of a testator whose will bequeathes amounts of $100, $50, and $10 respectively to three heirs in circumstances where his estate comes to merely 150. Since the estate falls short by $10/160 = 6.3$ percent, the three claimants would have to settle for roughly $94, $47, and $9, respectively. No doubt the alternative distribution of $90, $50, $10, respectively, would prevail in a majority vote, but this again goes to show no more than that impartial justice is not always the most popular course.

However, the issue may become still more problematic. An *economy of insufficiency* exists where the available resources are inadequate to satisfy all legitimate claims. But more drastic yet is an *economy of dire scarcity* where there is not "enough to go around" because if each party were to receive a "share proportional to his claims and deserts" then *everyone* would be pressed beneath the floor of a minimally acceptable level. Here one would surely not insist on proportionality when this would mean extinction for all.

This sort of situation is evident in such examples as the shortfall of kidneys available for transplantation with a group of otherwise well-qualified recipients. Since here there is simply not enough to go around in the case of an indivisible and unshareable good, there is no really plausible alternative short of random allocation.[3]

In such cases where there is a dire insufficiency—where equal shares pushes everyone beneath the level of an acceptable minimum—allocation by equal shares is unreasonable. Such a situation requires abandonment of straightforward proportionalism in distribution if catastrophe is to be avoided.

But, in fact, a less-then-obvious proportionalism is actually on the scene once we look at the issue in a different, more appropriate perspective. For the fact of it is that what all these parties have a claim to here is not an equal share of the commodity at issue but rather an equal opportunity to avert disaster. Fairness can still be realized by equal chances of securing that acceptable minimum—that is to say by indirect means. So here proportionalizing once again serves to engender equalization—not, to be sure, of commodity-shares as such, but of the chances of obtaining a minimally adequate share. Proportionism can still be maintained obliquely and so defended as the reasonable course.

Again, some theorists suggest that the problem of a surplus—a "windfall" creates problems for claim-proportionality fairness. Thus, consider the situation of the testator whose will reads: "I bequeathe the whole of my estate—whose value stands at $600—to my three nephews. A is to get $100, B is to get $200, and C is to get $300."

However, by the time of that testator's death his estate has appreciated to $1,200 so that a windfall of $600 is available for the beneficiaries. By claim proportionality fairness the three parties would get 200, 400, and 600, respectively, while by the process of equal division each would get $400, which may seem more appropriate.

However, it seems plausible to argue that in such windfall cases, claims function in a somewhat more complex way with the result that a *mixed* distribution process is actually appropriate. The base amount, here represented by that specified $600, is to be allocated by fairness/proportionality. But the resulting windfall of $600 is something on which all, in fact, have an equal claim so that the initial allocation is then to be supplemented by a division of the windfall on the basis of strict equality. In this event, our three claimants would obtain $300, $400, and $500, respectively, the windfall of $600 being divided equally between them. Despite its seeming abandonment of claim proportionality fairness, this division is, in fact, easily reconciled with that principle. For once the base amount is distributed proportionally to honor those documented claims, the residual windfall is (so it can plausibly be contended) something to which all the parties actually have equal claims, so that proportionality itself requires equality at this stage.

The long and short of it is that those seeming departures from claim-proportionality fairness that may seem appropriate in cases of shortfall and windfall are all readily reconciled to the demands of strict fairness. Such obstacles cannot block our path here. Are there others that can?

Notes

1. Brams and Taylor 1996, pp. 1-2.
2. In theory there is also the principle of *Earlier Claim Precedence*, which actually has more to be said on its behalf than *Larger-Claim Precedence* does. For example, when a firm goes bankrupt and its assets are insufficient to meet its liabilities, it makes sense that the earlier claims of its creditors should take precedence over later ones. For earlier on, the economic condition of the firm was less apparent, and the later creditors presumably had more time and ampler information about their decision to advance credit. Since they (presumably) ran these risks with open eyes, they should be prepared to take the consequences in stride and run a greater risk of loss. In fact, another time-conditioned variant of fairness, namely first-come-first-served is often used in practice. (Seats on buses and trains.)
3. See Rescher 1969.

4

Going Beyond Fairness?
Subjective Equity and Benevolent Allocation

(1) Equality in point of subjective evaluation is something very different from fairness. (2) In consequence, while a paternalism concerned to optimize the subjective equity of distributions may sometimes make good social and economic sense, it is something very different from fairness. (3) The best way to proceed with paternalistically benign distributions is by way of max-value equity. (4) Many sorts of examples illustrate this fact. (5) And this works as well for distributions of negativities as with positivities. (6) Mistaking one's valuations in the case of subjectively based allocations is not a good policy. (7) Nevertheless, there is no good reason to give much respect to merely subjective evaluations. And where justice is concerned, subjective equity is no substitute for fairness. Considerations of subjective evaluation may be crucial for economics, *but with* justice *they are beside the point.*

1. Subjective Evaluation and Pragmatic Equity

The impartiality that is crucial to fairness requires the use of objective standards. Fairness is a matter of *objective equity*—that is, the claim proportionality of shares, with their value determined on objective principles, without reference to the idiosyncratic, subjective, personalized evaluation of those involved. Benevolence, by contrast, seeks to accommodate the personal evaluations of individuals and to indulge their own characteristic preferences. (It is in this sense congenial to the tendency of modern economics, with its inclination towards mere preferences rather than some sort of objective valuation.)

In this context, evaluative objectivity need not and should not be construed in an transcendental or metaphysical sense. Rather, what it portends is depersonalized independence of the potentially idiosyncratic preferences of individuals or groups. What is at issue is the evaluative stance of the wider community of disinterested but well-informed individuals in a way that transcends the predilections and prejudices of particular individuals and groups. Market value rather than sentimental attachments or personal involvements is the crux.

Benevolence, by contrast, honors individual preferences. Now as regards personal evaluations, someone who would not be prepared to commit resources correspondingly if they could afford it cannot be said to attach great (subjective) value to something. You endow with subjective value only that for which you are, in principle, prepared to pay an objective price. To be sure, one may be *unable* to pay the price but one must not be *unwilling* to do so. To determine the subjective evaluations of individuals it is accordingly plausible to proceed by means of silent auctions—using fixed amounts of virtual money ("Monopoly Money") when it is desirable to put the issue of preexisting individual wealth aside. The use of sealed bids in a "blind (or silent) auction" is a natural means for determining the personal (subjective) evaluations of individuals that has become a standard method of evaluation.[1]

In any case, *distributive fairness* requires more than mere equity, mere share proportionality as such; it also requires that those shares be evaluated objectively. Thus let A and B be two equally entitled claimants for the distribution of some good a which for reasons of personal attachment they subjectively value as follows:

Item	Market Value	Value to A	Value to B
a	10	24	12

Fairness calls for allocating such a good so that each claimant gets the same objective value (which may, of course, require a resort to side payments). Thus in the present case a fair allocation will be either

To A	To B
$a - 5$	5

or the other way around—the matter is one of indifference, the objective value, inherent in a market-value appraisal, being the same either way.

So much for fairness. However, distributive equalization works quite differently at the subjective level. For on the basis of an equal *subjective* entitlement, A deems himself entitled to half of *a* which he values at 12 while B comparably deems himself due half of *a* which he values at only 6. On this basis, A's claim-proportionate share stands to B's on the ratio of 2:1. So now if *a* is allocated to A (who values it at 24) then fair-share proportionality from A's standpoint will have him pay a compensation of 12 to B. The resultant situation is

To A	To B
$a - 12 \cong 12$	12

Observe, however, that if the allocations were made to B the results would be

To A	To B
6	$a - 6 \cong 6$

This is obviously a suboptimal situation from the standpoint of both claimants alike. When distributions are made with reference to subjective evaluations, it is clearly appropriate to allot goods to those who set the highest value on them. The two approaches obviously lead to very different results.

Some distributive justice theorists put great stress on the idea of envy-freedom—the condition that obtains when no recipient would rather have the share of another. But it should be noted that a division could be envy-free and yet both objectively and subjectively inequitable. For consider a distribution of three atomistically indivisible items (*a-c*) to three equally deserving claimants (*A-C*) whose evaluations are as follows:

Item	Market value	Valuation by		
		A	B	C
a	40	60	50	50
b	30	50	70	50
c	20	50	50	1,000

Allotting each item to the individual who values it the most, produces the distribution A:a, B:b, C:c—which is obviously envy-free, since no recipient prefers the share of another. Nevertheless this distribution is neither objectively fair nor subjectively equitable. Achieving either desideratum would require side-payments to be made (albeit in opposite directions).

This example also conveys a larger lesson. When items have two different *kinds* of value (as with market value and subjective value in this example), then the situation can become such that *the realization of distributive equity with respect to both factors concurrently is a desideratum that may simply be unrealizable.* For example, if certain onerous tasks that must be done by a group are seen as having a price *both* in terms of time and in terms of effort, then it may prove impossible to effect a distribution of tasks that is equitable in both respects at once.

Various recent writers on distributive justice have characterized distributions as *superfair* when for all of the claimants involved they are preferable to a strictly fair distribution.[2] Such superfairness arises, for example, when three differently inclined parties are to share nine books—3 mysteries, 3 histories, and 3 romantic novels—and instead of the strictly fair distribution of one of each type per recipient, they all get three of the type they like best. Such a superfair distribution is more "efficient" (in the economists' sense) than one that is strictly fair because it enhances the "utility" (i.e., subjective satisfaction) of each of the parties involved. And moreover it effects a result where no-one has any reason to envy the shares received by the others because each has the share that he himself deems superior to theirs.

With fairness we are necessarily concerned for the claim-proportional division of goods. With superfairness, by contrast, we cast equity to the winds to suit the wishes of the parties at issue. Accordingly, when we shift from objectivity to subjective evaluations we actually change the topic. We no longer deal with fairness, as such, but at most with its distant cousin, subjective equity at issue with benevolence. When we take the subjective evaluations of individuals into account—their idiosyncratic tastes—we enter an arena of considerations different from justice.

There is, to be sure, one possible way of objectifying subjective values. That is to see the evaluations of the claimants as constituting

Going Beyond Fairness? Subjective Equity and Benevolent Allocation

a mini-market, a (virtual) market in which the value of items is determined. With *these* values then distributed in the usual claim-proportionate way we achieve a virtual fairness of sorts. We shall have occasion to return to this view of the matter below.

2. Subjective Equity and Paternalism

A distribution of any sort of value (subjective or otherwise) is *equitable* if it is claim-proportionate. As an aspect of impartial justice, fairness differs crucially from subjective equity, since with fairness one's concern is for the equitable distribution of impersonal or interpersonal ("objective") value. With subjective equity one tries to achieve a distribution that equitably accomodates the personalized and potentially idiosyncratic evaluations of the individuals involved.

Consider an example. Suppose that four items (a, b, c, d) are to be allocated to two equally entitled individuals (A and B) who for sentimental reasons value some of them in excess of their mere market value. The evaluations at issue are to be as follows:

Item	Market Value	Valuation by A	Valuation by B
a	10	15	30
b	20	25	20
c	15	40	15
d	15	15	25

The following distribution is perfectly equitable (i.e., claim-proportionate):

A: $a + b$ (market value 30; to-A value 40)

B: $c + d$ (market value 30; to-B value 40)

By their own valuation each party now secures a total of 40. However, a superior equitable distribution of *subjectively personalized* value would be:

A: $b + c$ (market value 35; to-A value 65)

B: $a + d$ (market value 25; to-B value 65)

However, this subjectively equitable and indeed universally preferred distribution is not objectively fair since it fails to establish equity with respect to the objective evaluations at issue. (If an allocator made that initial fair distribution, the parties could make deals to enhance their subjective position. But doing this is their business, not his.)

When making those economically efficient, utility-maximizing allocations one does not need—and indeed cannot really use—an impartial standard of value. Every claimant is allowed to make his own valuation. And these self-generated (and potentially idiosyncratic) valuations then serve as a basis of a paternalistically benevolent but still equitable distribution which nevertheless may fail to do justice to the demands of objective fairness. Accordingly, a particularly interesting category of distributions are those which are *paternalistically benevolent* in that, in the spirit of utilitarianism, they are concerned for maximizing the subjective value that results, while nevertheless striving for equity by distributing this in a claim-proportionate way. The example we have just considered illustrates this situation.

It is clear that paternalistic benevolence on the basis of subjective evaluations is something critically different from strict fairness which is concerned for the equitable distribution of objective values. Paternalistic benevolence thus has two conjoint objectives, generosity and equity: it seeks to maximize the subjective value of what is being distributed and concurrently to equalize the extent to which the subjective evaluations and preferences of the individuals concerned are accommodated. By contrast, fairness is impersonal—in implementing the demands of impartial justice it calls for ignoring the idiosyncratic preferences of people and opting for equal treatment on the basis of objective evaluations.

To be sure, from the subjective angle of the recipients, a benevolently equitable allocation is generally preferable to strict fairness. If you and I are to share two large cakes, one vanilla and one chocolate, then a fair division would call for half of each kind to each one of us. But clearly if you liked chocolate and disliked vanilla whereas my value scheme was the exact reverse then both would profit by your taking the whole of chocolate cake, and my taking the whole of vanilla.

Since paternalistic benevolence often benefits everyone, one may well ask what is wrong with it? As such—not much. Nothing in fact, apart from its abandonment of fairness. But that this is a negativity becomes clear through the following considerations. The idea of a fair price is one of the fundamental aspects of the conception of fairness. It is one of the fundamental principles of this domain that it is unfair to ask a higher price of one person than another simply because they have a greater need or want for the item at issue. But this is exactly what is what one does in the pursuit of subjective equity. Thus consider a case in which there are two (equally situated) heirs to an estate of two (indivisible) items of value, and consider the following two alternative valuations of these items:

Item	Market Value	Valuation I by A	by B	Valuation II by A	by B
a	100	100	100	100	100
b	100	100	200	100	300

And now consider the allocation of a to A and b to B. Subject to Valuation I this provides A with 100 subjective-value units and B with 200. For equalization under the aegis of paternalistic equity a charge of 50 will then be imposed on B in the interests of making his most-favored item available to him without comparatively disadvantaging A. But in the case of Valuation II this charge would increase to 100. As this example shows, with distributions that realize subjective equity there will be an increase in the cost of items to recipients who value them most. It is this consideration relating to the conception of a "fair price" operative with all alike that intrudes itself between subjective equity and fairness.

When our distributions take benign account of the preferences and idiosyncratic valuations that the recipients attach to the items at issue, we may indeed be heeding the siren call of benevolence—or even of worldly realism and economics—but we are no longer honoring the demands of fairness and impartial justice among whose most fundamental principles is that of a fair and person-indifferent price—of charging and crediting everyone alike for the same value for the same item. As Aristotle emphasized long ago, the balance that lies at the core of the ideas of justice and fairness cannot be achieved in the absence of impersonal and objective standards.

Still, despite its failure to honor the demands of abstract fairness, of course no-one would call such a paternalistically equitable distribution that honors the preferences of the recipients *unfair*. In fact, it is neither fair nor unfair, but *non-fair* in that when benevolence enters in we move outside the relevancy-range of fairness. We now change the topic from justice to welfare economics. In consequence, while a paternalism concerned to optimize the subjective equity of distributions may make good social and economic sense, it is something very different from fairness.

3. Paternalistic Benevolence in Distribution: The Advantages of Allocation by Max-Value Equity

Equity obviously cannot be achieved without evaluating the items being distributed. But just how should this evaluation be made?

Consider an indivisible item a whose value to three equally entitled claimants stand as follows:

Item	Market Value	Value to A	B	C
a	6	9	12	15

By hypothesis a's claim is to one-third of A. But we now have to decide how a's value is to be assessed in the context of a distribution. Here there are three plausible possibilities, seeing that the value at issue may be:

1. *Objective value* by impersonal standards (i.e., market value), namely 6 in the present case.

2. *Value-to-self* (personal value) in which event there is not just one answer, but three, namely:

    to-A value: 9
    to-B value: 12
    to-C value: 15

3. *Max-value*, that is value to the potential recipient who values it most highly. In the present case this would be 15.

At this point we confront the question: What is the equitable way to distribute a among these claimants? Given that equity calls for the claim-proportional distributions of the item being divided—or its equivalent value—we now obtain different answers to this question:

I. *Objective-Value Equity* (= Fairness).

The item is to be allocated to A, B, or C randomly, and the recipient pays 2 to each of his rivals. The result is that an objective value of 2 is realized for each claimant.

II. *Personal Equity* (= Pseudo-fairness)

Each claimant lays claim to a claim-proportionate share *at his own personal valuation*. And the allocation is now made on this (personal- or subjective-value) basis.

On this second approach, an item is to be alloted to the highest bidder, who must then make side-payments to assure proportionality *to the subjectively evaluated claims* of those involved. Thus in the present case we have it that it is allocated to C, who then makes side-payments of x to A and y to B in such a ways that

$$\frac{x}{\frac{1}{3}(9)} = \frac{y}{\frac{1}{3}(12)} = \frac{15-x-y}{\frac{1}{3}(15)}$$

Solving this pair of equations for x and y we obtain:

$x = 3.8$

$y = 5$

Accordingly we arrive at the subjective-value distribution:

A	B	C
3.8	5.0	$a - 8.8 \cong 6.2$

Here C, who prizes the item most, now receives the lion's share of value. What we have here is an allocation process that is characterized in the literature as "Knaster's procedure" which is predicated on the view that a claimant's equitable division is a matter of getting a claim-proportionate share of the overall value of these items with these claims assessed *as the claimant himself evaluates them*.³ (Observe that this procedure is not "envy-free" in equal-entitlement conditions; while neither rival would prefer having C's share, but A would certainly rather have B's.)

III. *Max-Value Equity*.

The' item is allocated to the claimant who values it maximally, and the resultant to-recipient value is then distributed claim-proportionately by the use of side-payments.

In the present case, by allocating the item a to the highest bidder, namely C, we realize a value of 15. By hypothesis all three claimants are entitled to share equally in a or its equivalent value. From an impartial point of view, each recipient becomes entitled to a one-third share of the value realized, which leads to the following result:

	Value to		
Item	A	B	C
a	5	5	$a - 10 \cong 5$

Each claimant now gets an equal share of the item's value as determined by its recipient—the one who prizes it the most. (The process is accordingly "envy-free.")

As these deliberations indicate, all three of these allocation procedures can lay claim to value-distribution equity. But it is, or should be, clear that procedure No. III—namely max-value equity—has the strongest case for equity with distributions based on subjective evaluations. For one thing, it is the simplest, most natural, and easiest to implement, requiring a minimum of information and calculation. But it is also the most sensible, seeing that it simply takes the overall value created by the most favorable allocation and distributes it in a straightforwardly equitable (share-proportionate) way.

In contrast with procedure No. I, No. III is bound to leave some recipients better satisfied by taking a more generous view. And in contrast with procedure No. II, No. III is envy-free: no claimant can

Going Beyond Fairness? Subjective Equity and Benevolent Allocation

have any reason to prefer the share of another. Moreover, No II is involved in the very questionable supposition that a higher valuation should earn a higher share. Max-value equity thus lays claim to distributive appropriateness in combining equity with generosity since it puts everyone on the same footing relative to the most generous evaluation of the claim at issue. After all, the bidding winner already enjoys the advantage of securing the desirable item at issue; there is no real reason why he should get a lion's share of value besides.

For these reasons we shall here employ the max-value equity process at issue in procedure No. III as the standard method for allocating differentially valued indivisible goods. After all, this process also extends easily—and naturally—to the case of the distribution of a plurality of goods. For here we can proceed seriatim, allocating each component of the overall compound distribution separately, step by step.

For example, suppose that a legacy of a thousand dollars and two watches and $1,000 has been left by a deceased relation to two siblings, A and B on equal terms. And suppose further that the evaluative situation is as follows:

Item	Market Value	Value to A	Value to B
Watch 1	$500	$500	$800
Watch 2	$50	$100	$50
$1,000	$1,000	$1,000	$1,000

To maximize the distribution of value here we proceed to regard these subjective values as bids in a silent auction and allocate the items concerned to the high bidder. For equity, however, we must then require this awardee to compensate the looser by an amount suitable for establishing claim proportionality. Thus in the present case we have:

	Allocation to A	Allocation to B
Watch 1 Division	$400	$w_1 - \$400 \cong 400$
Watch 2 Division	$w_2 - 50 \cong 50$	50
$1,000 division	500	500
TOTAL	$w_2 + 850 \cong 950$	$w_1 + 150 \cong 950$

Observe that in such cases an allocation that is item-wise equitable must result in collectively equitable allocation.

To be sure, awarding a contested item on the basis of max-value equity may well lead to the item's going to the person who has the smallest claim to it. Thus, for example, consider the following case of a distribution where A has a claim to 1/100, B one of 2/100, and C one of 97/100, but where these three parties value the item a at issue as follows:

	Value to		
Item	A	B	C
a	100	10	1

By allocating the item to A, we realize a value of 100. He accordingly gets a to-A value of 100 and is entitled to 1/100 of this, viz., 1, and so pays 99 to his rivals. B with his 2/100 share gets 2, and the remaining 97 go to C with his lion's share of 97/100. Here the item goes to A—the least-share claimant who values it the most. And so C, whose claim is the largest, fails to get the contested item—but does get ample compensation.

The question arises: How is one to understand max-value equity to work in situations where there are side conditions that limit the range of available distributions? Suppose, for example, that three items (a, b, c) are being allocated to three individuals (A, B, C) subject to the stipulative condition that each is to get exactly one of them. And let it be that they value these items as follows:

	Value to		
Item	A	B	C
a	15	12	9
b	15	9	9
c	9	9	8

Ordinarily we would assign both a and b to A on max-value grounds, but now A is only eligible to receive one of them, so this option is unavailable. All the same, what is to be done in such a case on the basis of max-value equity is clear. We begin with a survey of

Going Beyond Fairness? Subjective Equity and Benevolent Allocation

all the eligible options, namely all of the possible allocations that meet those restrictive stipulative conditions that are at issue:

	A	B	C	Total Value
	a	b	c	32
	a	c	b	33
	b	a	c	35
	b	c	a	33
	c	a	b	30
	c	b	a	27

Of all of the eligible allocations it is $A{:}b$, $B{:}a$, $C{:}c$ that yields the largest total of value (viz. 35), and it would, accordingly, be this distribution that would serve as the basis for the determination of shares, as follows:

	A	B	C
a	$+4$	$a-8$	$+4$
b	$b-10$	$+5$	$+5$
c	$+2\frac{2}{3}$	$+2\frac{2}{3}$	$c-5\frac{2}{3}$
TOTAL	$b-3\frac{1}{3} \cong 11\frac{2}{3}$	$a-\frac{1}{3} \cong 2\frac{2}{3}$	$c+3\frac{2}{3} \cong 11\frac{2}{3}$

This distribution yields the equitably maximal result through its equal division of the maximum that is realizable (viz. 35).

The process of max-value allocation in such cases is thus straightforward. When side-conditions are imposed we first determine the value-maximizing alternative(s) among the eligible distributions and then proceed in the standard way to make the item-wise equitable distribution on that basis.

It should be observed that an equitable distribution even when supplemented by subsequent trading may not yield an optimal result from the angle of the parties involved. Consider an example. Three equally valuable ee heirs (A, B, C) have equal claims upon an estate consisting of six objects that they evaluate differently:

Item	Market Value	Valuation by A	B	C
a	9	10	9	20
b	9	10	9	20
c	9	20	10	9
d	9	20	10	9
e	9	9	20	10
f	9	9	20	10

Let us begin with the perfectly fair distribution $a + b$ to A, $c + d$ to B, and $e + f$ to C. No trades are possible here because no *pairwise* (non-multilateral) exchange of items can advantage both parties in terms of their own valuations. Nevertheless, the from-the-ground-up redistribution of $c + d$ to A; $c + f$ to B; $a + b$ to C would significantly advantage all concerned.

The lesson here is straightforward: "If you make a fair distribution and count on the parties who are not fully content to make trading revisions among themselves, then in the end you may not do as well by the parties as an impartial arbiter would be able to do for them." Accordingly, in some circumstances people will fare better in a benevolent allocation than they could possibly do for themselves as independent agents making pairwise trades on their own. (Of course, it might be said that this is simply the price people have to pay for being treated as adults rather than having their affairs managed paternalistically.)

4. Further Examples

Suppose that three students agree to share the year's lease of a house with three bedrooms, with each to have one of the bedrooms while the other rooms (kitchen, living room, etc.) to be shared in common. The bedrooms differ in point of desirability (in relation to size, view, quietness, etc.) The overall rent for the house is $900 per month. How should this be shared out in view of those differen-

Going Beyond Fairness? Subjective Equity and Benevolent Allocation 69

tially valuable bedrooms? The available options include such perfectly fair procedures as:

1. Allocate bedrooms by lot
2. Rotate room occupancy every two or three months

However, these processes may fail to yield a generally acceptable result, and there is yet another alternative that takes account of the factor of personalized valuation. The idea here is to auction off the first and second choice of bedrooms.

To begin with each sharer owes \$300 towards that overall rental of \$900. Then when the right of first choice is auctioned off, it turns out to be worth \$200 to A and less to B and C. And thereupon the right of second refusal is worth \$100 to B and less to C. So A gets first pick and B the next, thereby raising a supplemental surplus of \$300 which is divided evenly among the parties since the claims for this asset are equal. The resulting overall rental is

A: $-300 - 200 + 100 = -400$

B: $-300 - 100 + 100 = -300$

C: $-300 - 0 + 100 = -200$

Thus A pays extra for the privilege of first choice, and C gets compensation for being low man on the totem pole.

Again, consider the case of four items being shared out among three equally entitled claimants who value these items as follows:

Item	Value to A	B	C
a	10	8	21
b	12	12	21
c	12	6	4
d	24	22	20

Proceeding in the by now familiar way of subjective-value maximizing equity we would base our division in the following calculation:

	Allocation to		
Item	A	B	C
a	7	7	$a - 14$
b	7	7	$b - 14$
c	$c - 8$	4	4
d	$d - 16$	8	8
TOTAL	$c + d - 10$	+26	$a + b - 16$

But now suppose that we were constrained to proceed without any side payments. Then we would begin by surveying all of the possible distributions that let no one individual fall below some plausible amount—in the present case, say 20:

	Number 1	Number 2
A:	$b + c$ (24)	$a + c$ (22)
B:	d (22)	d (22)
C:	a (21)	b (21)

Since distribution No. 1 dominates No. 2, it is now the best that we can do. The total value distributed now comes to 67 instead of that initial $3 \times 26 = 78$. Here, as elsewhere, it is clear that accommodating restrictive conditions can exact a price.

Consider the following example that has been discussed in the literature.[4] Four items of value a, b, c, d constitute an estate that is to be divided among three equally qualified heirs, who evaluate these items as follows:

Going Beyond Fairness? Subjective Equity and Benevolent Allocation

Item	Value to A	Value to B	Value to C
a	$10,000	$4,000	$7,000
b	2,000	1,000	4,000
c	500	1,500	2,000
d	800	2,000	1,000
TOTAL	$13,300	$8,500	$14,000

The only side-condition here is that each heir is to get at least one item.

In effecting a division here we can then proceed seriatim, item by item, along the lines of the max-value equity approach, allotting each item to the highest bidder with the others compensated by a side-payment for equalization:

Item	Allocation to A	Allocation to B	Allocation to C
a	$a - 6{,}667$	3,333	3,333
b	1,333	1,333	$b - 2{,}667$
c	667	667	$c - 1{,}333$
d	667	$d - 1{,}333$	667
TOTAL	$a - 4000$	$d + 4{,}000$	$b + c$

Observe that this allocation not only effects the greatest possible distribution of value but also is envy-free: no claimant would prefer the share of another since each values his share at 6,000 and that of the others at less.

An alternative line of approach that has been suggested in the literature[5] would be to proceed as follows. The three heirs, A, B, C value the estate at 13,300; 8,500; and 14,000 respectively and deem themselves duly entitled to one third of it, namely 4,433, 2,833, and 4,667 respectively. Thus by the preceding max-bidder distribution which gives each a value of 6,000, they would receive an excess of 1,577, 3,477, and 1,333, respectively, creating an overall surplus of 6,387. But—so the proposed reasoning runs—the excess should be distributed equally at 2,129 apiece. Hence B who gets the lion's share of the excess at 3,477 ought to pay out 1,348 with 555 going to A and 796 going to C. On this basis, the ultimate division would become:

A: $a - 4{,}000 + 555$ = $a - 3{,}445 \cong 6{,}555$ (to-A)

B: $d + 4{,}000 - 1{,}348$ = $d + 2{,}652 \cong 4{,}652$ (to-D)

C: $b + c + 796$ = $b + c + 796 \cong 6{,}796$ (to-C)

It is clear that the side-payments operative here differ somewhat from the results of the max-value equity approach, with the net effect that B, whose expectations were a good deal more modest, winds up with a stake of significantly diminished value at the expense of the others. (That this serves the interests of fairness is far from clear.)

Most theorists who have approached this particular problem of fair division from the angle of economics or decision theory have opted for a resolution somewhat along these "surplus"-dividing lines. Nevertheless, however satisfied or dissatisfied the parties involved might be on the basis of this distribution—and it is hard to see why B should be content with his comparatively disadvantaged lot—it is certainly not something that a benevolent and neutral outsider would consider imposing on the group.

One associated advantage of max-value distribution is that on its basis the claimants have very little incentive to misrepresent their valuations. Since the auction is closed, they would be ill-advised to undervalue those dividenda since they thereby put their chance to get them at risk. On the other hand, they have good reason not to overprice those items since they thereby risk obtaining them subject to having to make an inflated payoff to their rivals.[6]

For an instructive example, consider the situation of three equally entitled claimants (A - C) in a distribution of six objects (a-f) whose value they themselves appraise as follows:

Going Beyond Fairness? Subjective Equity and Benevolent Allocation 73

Item	Value to		
	A	B	C
a	100	50	50
b	100	50	120
c	50	100	50
d	120	100	50
e	50	50	100
f	50	120	100

And now consider the allocations:

No. I
$A: a + b$ — To-recipient value 200
$B: c + d$ — 200
$C: e + f$ — 200

This distribution is envy-free: no recipient would fare better by having the share of another. Nevertheless there is a different (subjectively equitable) distribution that all recipients would prefer to this one, namely:

No. II
$A: a + d$ — To-recipient value 220
$B: c + f$ — 220
$C: e + b$ — 220

This finding is arrived at as follows. Proceeding by the process of max-value distribution we have:

Item	Allocation to		
	A	B	C
a	$a - 66$	33	33
b	40	40	$b - 80$
c	33	$c - 66$	33
d	$d - 80$	40	40
e	33	33	$e - 66$
f	40	$f - 80$	40
TOTAL	$a + d$	$c + f$	$b + e$

In this instance we have a perfectly even distribution where the side-payments cancel out.

A multi-item allocation of this sort, which achieves equity (claim-proportionality) without any side payments may be called *even*—and otherwise uneven. When a distribution is at one and the same time both evaluatively maximal and even, it is *subjectively perfect*—and otherwise subjectively imperfect. Distribution No. II constitutes an example of subjective perfection.

5. Negativities

One vivid illustration of fairness in matters of distributing an onus is afforded by the graduated income tax. The very different levels of renumeration all come into operation in ascending order here: the level of basic adequacy, of comfort, of affluence, and of riches, respectively. (These levels may be taken to correspond to something like one-half the average person's income, fully the average, twice the average, and ten times the average, respectively.) A graduated income tax establishes different brackets for the sake of distributive fairness and in a developed economy the corresponding tax brackets will come to something like 0 percent, 10 percent, ~25 percent, and ~33 percent, respectively. Of course, these various figures are not fixed by considerations of general principle; they issue (ideally) from a careful analysis of the social context in point of funding public revenue needs, providing for adequate social services creating disincentives to investment, and so on.

The same distribution processes that we have been discussing will work with bads as well as goods. Let us return to the housekeeping example discussed at p. 39 above and consider three parties (A, B, C) who have to divide three tasks:

a = shopping & cleaning

b = cooking

c = dishwashing & garbage removal

A plausible way of proceeding subjectistically is to give each sharer 100 onus points to allocate to these tasks in line with the extent of his distaste for it. For the sake of discussion suppose that the result is as follows:

Going Beyond Fairness? Subjective Equity and Benevolent Allocation

	Onus Allocation by		
Item	A	B	C
a	−50	−40	−35
b	−40	−30	−35
c	−10	−30	−30

So for starters we have the distribution which gives each party their most favored (least disfavored) choice:

$A{:}c$ at   −10

$B{:}b$ at   −30

$C{:}a$ at   −35

For onus equalization we will charge A an amount x and B an amount y, with these amounts so adjusted as to make for equality all around. The respective share will then be

A: $-10 - x$

B: $-30 - y$

C: $-35 + x + y$

A bit of calculation shows that to assure equality we will need to have:

$x = 15$ and $y = -5$

The result is an even-steven distribution of onus (at -25 points each).

The upshot is that A gets away with the least onerous task but must compensate his partners.

To be some concrete implementation of this process requires determining the value of an onus point. Since we are trying for an impartial process that treats *all* of the parties alike we shall treat the onus of each strictly alike. If hiring a maid to do *all* the work comes to $180 per week, the value of those 75 onus points would be $-2.40 each. Thus A would compensate B by $2.40 × 5 = $12 per week and C by $2.40 × 10 = $24 per week.

Alternatively, the compensation could be made in labor rather than cash. This invites the following line of thought.

- A owes B 5 onus points, which he will pay off by taking on 1/6 th of B's task of doing b.

- A owes C 10 onus points which he will pay off by taking over 2/7 th of C's task of doing a.

6. Unreasonable and/or Deceptive Valuations

When an allocation is made on the basis of subjective values, can the claimants involved gain by cheating? Consider an example. Two indivisible items (a, b) are to be allocated as between two claimants (A, B), with subsequent adjustments for equity in recognition of an equal entitlement. And let it be that the following evaluations obtain:

	Market Value	Valuation by A Actual	Valuation by A Professed	Valuation by B Actual & Professed
a	100	250	150	200
b	200	200	300	250
c	250	300	220	200

As regards a, claimant A simply loses out by underplaying his valuation and B gets the item that he (A) should properly have had. As regards b, by overvaluing this item A gets it at the price of an overpayment: he pays more for b than he thinks its worth and has to compensate B with a payment of 5 to boot. As regards c, A does actually benefit by his underevaluation and winds up paying B only 10 rather than 50. Nevertheless, even if he had been honest he would still have obtained this item for substantially less than it was worth to him. And by misstating his valuation he took a real risk of the sort of mishaps that afflicted him in the case of a and b.

Going Beyond Fairness? Subjective Equity and Benevolent Allocation

Again suppose that 12 litres of wine are to be shared out among three equally qualified claimants who value the wine differently. Then as the situation of display 1 indicates, undervaluing the wine can manage to increase one's share. Note, however, that, if the recipient is kept uncertain as to whether he will receive his share in money or in goods, then the temptation to fake his true valuation is removed thanks to the risks of loss.

Display 1
Diversity in Evaluation

	Case 1		Case 2		Case 3	
	Valuation	Shares (litres)	Valuation	Shares (litres)	Valuation	Shares (litres)
A	100	4	100	3	100	4.8
B	100	4	100	3	100	4.8
C	100	4	50	6	200	2.4

7. Affective Involvement

All of these considerations about subjective-value distributions notwithstanding, the fact remains that fairness' neglect of subjective values and idiosyncratic preferences is no negativity as far as considerations of justice are concerned. For subjective values can take us down some pretty odd pathways. For example, an interesting complication can arise through the prospects of an "auction of affective involvement." Such an auction introduces the complication that not only is the item being auctioned of some value to me, but if I should fail, then it has some value to me if X gets it—or it would require compensation to resign me to Y's getting it.

For the sake of an example, consider a case where A and C are hostile to one another while A and B are quite friendly, as are B and C. On this basis, we might then confront the following situation:

		If the item goes to		
Value to		A	B	C
A		1,200	400	−200
B		200	800	200
C		−300	300	1,200
	TOTAL	1,100	1,500	1,200

Here in giving the item to B we generate the (maximum) value of 1,500, seeing that C's resentment of A countervails against A's maximum bid. However, to equalize (at 500) the benefits that arise with a to-B allocation we would have to require B to pay out 300 (100 to A and 200 to C). Each party then gets a benefit of 500—in B's case through getting the contested item (albeit at a cost) and in A's and C's case through "sharing the wealth" and additionally getting some value from the satisfaction derived from a to-B allocation.

To be sure while such an approach seems benign it is nevertheless deeply problematic because of its validating endorsement of dislike and jealousy—a disadvantage it shares with any recourse to subjective valuation.

Thus consider a case where either of two parties would rather do without than see the other benefit. (They are prepared to "cut off their nose to spite their face" as the saying goes.) Suppose that in such a situation a sum of $1,000 is being divided between otherwise equal claimants who view each other with dislike. On this basis it pains A a dollars' worth to see a dollar go to B and similarly it pains B two dollars worth to see a dollar go to A. If $$x$ goes to A and thereby $1000 - x$ to B, we will have:

A's subjective valuation: $x - (1000 - x)$

B's subjective valuation: $(1000 - x) - 2x$

To achieve equalization we must thus have:

$2x - 1000 = 1000 - 3x$

As a result, $x = \$400$. Thus for psychic equalization in the face of B's more intense jealousy we have to deprive A of $100 (i.e., give her merely $400) in place of the $500 that would ordinarily be her due.

However, there is no good reason whatever why the rest should indulge B's antipathy and acknowledge the validity of her "claim." Subjective evaluation is not necessarily something that should be honored. The extent to which it deserves to be acknowledged in matters of distributive justice very much depends on the nature of the case.

8. A Lesson

The upshot of these deliberations is that subjective equity is something quite different from strict fairness. The former accommodates personal evaluations and idiosyncratic preferences, the latter proceeds in terms of impersonal valuations and objective preferabilities. Fairness as an aspect of impersonal justice has to proceed on the basis of objective value. If I have to make restitution to you for a broken vase, it must be on the basis of its market value—the special value you assign to it as a gift from a former sweetheart has to be left out of it. Where justice is concerned, the aspect of impersonal valuation becomes crucial and individual preferences must be dismissed from view. Paternalistic allocation based on subjective values is deeply problematic where considerations of justice are at issue because it allows claims to be based on considerations of affective involvement that should now be ignored.

The difference between fairness and people's advantage that is at issue here is crucial for the difference between two important human enterprises, namely justice and economics. As has been realized ever since Mandeville's classic *Fable of the Bees* this difference is vast and portentous. For the fact of it is that people's personal evaluations help to set matters into motion. Only if you prefer having my a while I prefer having your b will we trouble to make the exchange. If the only evaluation that came into it were one of impersonal value, the economic process would collapse. In economic transactions, subjectivity makes the world go round. But justice is something else again.

Those theorists who concern themselves with subjective equity and benevolent allocation do indeed deal with an issue of significance and importance. However, this significance and importance appertains to matters of economic paternalism rather than justice. To think—let alone *say*, as various theorists so glibly do—that this sort of thing addresses the issue of *fairness* is to hold a view that is profoundly mistaken because it fails to accord to considerations of impersonal justice the weight that is their due.

Notes

1. See Knaster 1946, Steinhaus 1948, Knaster and Steinhaus 1953.
2. The most elaborate and extensive treatment of superfairness is Baumol 1986. But see also Foley 1967, Pazner and Schnieder 1974, Varian 1974, and Yaari 1984. The

concept was reportedly introduced by the Dutch physicist Ehrenfest in the 1950's. (See Baumol 1986, p. 71.)
3. On Knaster's procedure see Brams and Tayor 1996, pp. 52-57.
4. Luce and Raiffa 1957, pp. 366-67; Raiffa 1982, pp. 290-91; Brams and Taylor 1996, pp. 52-55.
5. See Brams and Taylor 1996, pp. 52-55.
6. Moreover, an element of objectivity—or at least of interpersonality—enters into max-value pricing. Each participant can determine the size of his own valuation, but only the group-as-a-whole determines whose valuation is maximal.

5

Probabilistic Expectations

Dividing Prospective Gains in Risk Situations: The Historical Background

(1) Probabilistic proportionism calls for the allocation of shares in line with the mathematical expectation of the claimants. (2) Already in the seventeenth century, G. W. Leibniz proposed that this should be adopted as a general instrumentality of distributive justice. (3) And J. M. Keynes later joined Leibniz espousing such expected-value awards as a basis for settling conflicting claims in legal situations. (4) But is this really a tenable view of the issue?

Gottfried Wilhelm Leibniz's fascination with difficult legal issues dates from his early years and found expression in the doctoral dissertation, *De casibus perplexis in jure*, which he presented to the University of Altdorf at the tender age of twenty in 1666. This interest in law intersected with his concern for combinatorics and probability when, in a 1687 letter to Vincentius Placcius,[1] one of his longest-term correspondents, he wrote as follows: "If two litigants lay claim to a sum of money, and if the claim of the one is twice as probable as that of the other, the sum should be divided between them in that proportion."[2] In effect, the comparative size of the claim is to be measured by the probability of its validity on the basis of the evidence.

It can be seen, however, that such an endorsement of evidence-proportionate division is deeply problematic because it rests on an overly facile assimilation of the judicial allocation problem to the perhaps similar-seeming, but actually very different problem of fair division in gambling. Let us consider how this is so.

Suppose that a game of dice has reached a stage where only two players, *A* and *B*, remain as contenders, and where winning all or nothing is to be decided one way or the other by *A*'s getting three or five. But suppose further that the game has to be broken off at this point. How should the stakes constituting the "pot" now be divided between *A* and *B*?

Since *A*'s winning has the probability 1/3 and *B*'s the probability 2/3—so that *A*'s chances of winning are exactly half of *B*'s—it seems proper and sensible to divide the stake between them in the proportion 1:2. The guiding idea is that a just division can be based on exactly the proportionality principle that was contemplated in Leibniz's contention:

$$\frac{\text{proportionate share of } A}{\text{proportionate share of } B} = \frac{A\text{'s probability of winning}}{B\text{'s probability of winning}}$$

On this basis, the following relationship holds with respect to any one of the participants *X*:

$$\frac{\text{proportionate share of } X}{X\text{'s probability of winning}} = \text{constant}$$

In consequence we have it that:

proportionate share of *X* ~ *X*'s probability of winning.

And since the several proportionate shares must, in the aggregate, sum to the total stake at issue we then obtain:

proportionate share of *X* = *X*'s probabilistic expectation.

The approach at issue accordingly stipulates that in gambling situations a participant's appropriate share in the overall stake is to be simply the probabilistically determined *mathematical expectation* (expected value) of the gamble for this particular party.[3]

All of the claimants are to be treated similarly with respect to this principle. In this sense, the division is perfectly fair, seeing that an impersonal principle of allocation is uniformly in operation.[4] And exactly this indeed is the traditional resolution of the gambling division problem—the classical "problem of points" of sharing out the stake between the participants in a fair game that is stopped in midcareer.

It was, in fact, this general issue of the proper division of stakes for prematurely terminated games that provided the launching impetus to the development of the calculus of probability. Leibniz himself described the general situation in 1705 as follows:

> Mathematicians have begun, in our own day, to calculate the chances in games. It was the Chevalier de Méré—a man of acute mind, a gambler and philosopher, whose *Agreements* and other works have been published—who prompted them by raising questions about the division of stakes, wanting to know how much [a given player's part in] a game would be worth if this game were interrupted at such a point. Accordingly, he invited his friend M. Pascal to take a brief look at the problem. The question caused a stir and prompted M. Huygens to write his treatise on chance. Other learned men joined in. Certain principles were established, and were also employed by Pensionary De Witt in a little discourse, published in Dutch, on annuities. The foundation they built on involved *prosthaphaeresis*, i.e. arriving at an arithmetic mean between several equally admissible hypotheses. Our peasants have used this method for a long time, guided by their natural mathematics. For instance, when some inheritance or piece of land is to be sold, they appoint three teams of assessors—these teams are called *Schurzen* in Low Saxon—and each team assesses the commodity in question. Now suppose that the first estimates its value at 1,000 crowns, and second at 1,400 and the third at 1,500; they take the total of these three, which is 3,900, and because there were three teams they take a third of this, 1,300, as the mean value sought. Or, what comes to the same thing, they take the sum of one third of each estimate. This is the axiom: *aequalibus aequalia*—like hypotheses must receive like consideration. But when the hypotheses are unlike, we compare them with one another. Suppose, for instance, that with two dice one player will win if he throws a 7 and the other if he throws a 9. We want to know their relative likelihoods of winning. I say that the second player is only two thirds as likely to win as the first player, since there are three ways in which the first can throw a 7 with two dice—1 and 6, or 2 and 5, or 3 and 4—whereas there are only two ways in which the second can throw a 9, Namely by throwing 3 and 6, 4 and 5. And all these ways are equally possible, so that the likelihoods, which match the numbers of equal possibilities, will be as 3 to 2 or 1 to 2/3. I have said more than once that we need a new kind of logic, concerned with degrees of probability, since Aristotle in his *Topics* could not have been further from it: he was content to set out certain familiar rules, arranged according to the commonplaces—rules which may be useful in some contexts where a discourse has to be developed and given some likelihood—without taking the trouble to provide us with balances which are needed to weight likelihoods and to arrive at sound judgments regarding them.[5]

In his discussion of "mathematical expectation," which, he maintains, "is a technical expression originally derived from the scientific study of gambling and games of chance, and stands for the product of the possible gain with the probability of attaining it." John Maynard Keynes went so far as to credit Leibniz with originating this conception.[6] But this attribution is not really accurate, since the idea had certainly been used earlier by mathematical theorists in France (de Méré, Pascal, Fermat) and Holland (Huygens, de Witt)—in connection both with games of chance and with the economics of insurance. It would be more correct to say that while Leibniz did not *initiate* this idea, he promoted it beyond the level of earlier treatments, insisting that one should recognize expectation-based distribution as an instrument of vastly diversified applicability and utility.

A prime text for the exposition of his theory is Leibniz's essay *De incerti aestimatione*,[7] where he puts the salient point as follows:[8]

> If among all possible outcomes some yield the value A, others the value B, and the rest the value C, then the total expectation (*spes*) will be the sum of the several values multiplied by the number of all possible outcomes. Thus if the number of outcomes that can yield the value A is *a*, the number of outcomes the can yield the result B is *b*, and the number of outcomes that can yield the result C is *c*, and the number of all possible outcomes is *n*, then the expectation (*specs*) will be:

$$S = \frac{aA + bB + cC}{n}$$

Here, supposing equivalent outcomes—so that *a/n* is the probability of realizing the value A, *b/n* that of realizing B, and *c/n* that of realizing C—Leibniz's treatment of the issue makes it clear that expectation is the aggregate sum of the product of the probabilities of the several outcomes by their respective values.

Thus—to illustrate by an insurance example—if the probability of a ship's sinking in a storm during a certain voyage is one in a hundred, with the loss standing at 10,000 ducats on the outbound voyage and 40,000 ducats on the return voyage, then the overall effective magnitude of the misfortune of loss would be appraised at

(.01 x 1/2) x 10,000 + (.01 x 1/2) x 40,000

or 250 ducats, would accordingly represent an equitable measure of the magnitude of the negativity at issue ("a possible loss of our ship in a storm"), affording an appropriate basis for assessing the value of insurance.

1. Expectations Generalized

As such examples show, Leibniz was prepared to move well beyond the close connection between *expectation* and *equity* that characterized the thought of the other founders of probability theory. And it is interesting to see his fertile mind at work envisioning various applications for expected value allocations that are remote from its origin in the division of gambling stakes and the pricing of insurance such as annuities and land appraisals. Moreover, Leibniz also contemplates using the same approach with respect to medical prescriptions. If various (*ex hypothesi* equally competent) physicians prescribe different doses of a medication in a given case, we should again adopt the arithmetical mean.⁹ Again, he proposed to apply it in moral casuistry, subject to the idea that the appropriateness of an action will depend on two factors:

1. "safety"—the inherent moral appropriateness/ inappropriateness of an action's result

and

2. "probability"—the likelihood (relative to the evidence) of its being mandatory; the degree to which its requiredness can be established.

Thus, if an action has a low degree of safety because it is inherently morally questionable (e.g., abandoning one's family to lead a life of meditation and prayer) then a stronger rationale of validation will be needed to substantiate its appropriateness in given circumstances:

> And when our moralists—I mean the wisest of them, such as the present General of the Jesuits—bring in the question of what is safest as well as of what is most probable, and even put safety ahead of probability, they do not really abandon the most probable. For here the question of *safety* is the question of the *improbability of an impending evil*. Moralists who are lax about this have gone wrong largely because they have had an inadequate and over-narrow notion of probability, which they have confused with Aristotle's *endoxon* or *acceptability*: in his *Topics* Aristotle aimed only to conform to the opinions of other people, as did the orators and the Sophists. *Endoxon*, for him, is whatever is accepted by the greatest number or by the most authoritative; he was wrong to restrict his *Topics* to that, and this approach meant that he only concerned himself there with accepted maxims, most of them vague—as though wanting to reason by means of nothing but old jokes and proverbs. But probability or likelihood is broader—it must be drawn from the nature of things: and the opinion of weighty authorities is one of the things which can contribute to the likelihood of an opinion, but it does not produce the entire likelihood by itself.[10]

And so Leibniz viewed the principle of probabilistic proportionalism—the allocation of shares in line with mathematical expectation—as a general principle of ethical practice, able to provide appropriate guidance not just for the division of goods in gambling situations but to serve as a general instrumentality of distributive justice. Not only is probability the guide of life (as Bishop Butler put it), it is the guide of justice as well, seeing that mathematical expectations constitute the measure of fair shares.

On this basis, Leibniz proposed to use the expected-value approach in measuring the overall value of goods and evils within a broadly conceived moral calculus. Effectively, the overall magnitude of something good or bad should be measured by the *product* of its inherent value by the probability of its realization:

(inherent value) x (probability of eventuation).

Thus Leibniz went on to observe:

> The question of how inevitable a result is (*la grandeur de la consequence*, i.e., its likelihood) is heterogeneous from—i.e. cannot be compared with—the question of how good or bad it is (*la grandeur du consequent*, i.e., its value). So in trying to compare them, moralists have become muddled, as can be seen from writings on probability. The fact is that in this as in other assessments which are disparate, heterogeneous, and with more than one dimension (so to speak), the magnitude of the thing in question is made up proportionately of two estimates; as with a rectangle.[11]

As Leibniz saw it, the expected value idea of a multiplicative conjoining of probability and magnitude affords a tool of impressive versatility and power in the allocation of goods and evils in general. Where the early probabilists conceived of an instrument for dealing with games of chance and matters of insurance, Leibniz with his characteristic expansiveness of view envisioned a generalized resource for handling legal and moral claims an instrumentality of fairness across the board.

2. The Leibniz-Keynes Doctrine

Commenting on the expected-value principle as a basis for deciding legal conflicts regarding ownership, John Maynard Keynes joined Leibniz in endorsing it with the observation, "The doctrine seems sensible, but I am unaware that it has ever been acted on."[12] And so, as Leibniz and Keynes saw it, probabilistic expected-value evaluations afford the key to the general resolution of the problem of allocating fair shares in situations of uncertainty.

There is no doubt that probabilistically grounded distribution of goods often makes good common sense in matters of distributive justice. For example, insurance is a plausible instance of such an indirect, probabilistic way of sharing risks. Take automobile damage insurance. Driving a car is an economically and socially advantageous institution which nevertheless inflicts gross damage (both physical and monetary) on the thousands of people involved in accidents every year. There is no way of dividing the damage equally among those who benefit from the use of motor vehicles. The best that can be done is to distribute the economic losses in a way that is essentially probabilistic, through some such measures as legally mandatory liability insurance.

And, in general, it is clear that in many real-life situations allocation by probabilistic proportionalism is the proper way to proceed. Thus consider the following situation. Uncle John and Aunt Harriet have an estate of $300,000. John's will leaves everything to Harriet if she survives him, and otherwise divides his estate to cousin A and to cousin B. Harriet's will leaves everything to her husband John if he survives her, and otherwise divides her estate to cousin A and to cousin B. John and Harriet go off on a round-the-world trip but somewhere along the way they simply vanish. As the statutes specify, after 7 years both are presumed dead. But in settling the estate the crucial question is: who died first? Whose will is it that is to be operative? Given their ages and conditions of health it is likely that John—older and frailer of health—died first. So let p be the likelihood that he did. Then we have:

A inherits: $p \times 1/3 \, (300,000) + (1 - p) \times 2/3 \, (300,000) = 100,000 \, (2 - p)$
B inherits: $(1 - p) \times 1/3 \, (300,000) - p \times 2/3 \, (300,000) = 100,000 \, (1 + p)$

If p were $1/2$, they would divide that 300,000 evenly, but since the actuarial tables indicates (so we may presume) that is 3/4, A will inherit $125,000 and B will inherit $175,000, thus getting rather more than A because it is quite likely that Harriet's will prevails.

The Leibniz-Keynes approach is predicated on the principle of allocating to claimant a share that is proportional to their expectation, for example, partitioning 50:50 between two players who have an equal chance of winning. But if the mathematical expectations measured through chances of winning were an adequate measure of entitlements in general, then one would stand committed to the idea that where there is no difference in mathematical expectation there will be no difference in procedural appropriateness in matters of share allocation. And this means that we might as well award the whole dividendum probabilistically in a way that gives all claimants their share-proportionate expectation. On such an approach, the probability of securing the prize becomes tantamount to dividing the prize itself. But in contexts of distributive justice this is just not how matters work. A dollar in one's pocket is a sure-thing asset; a one-in-a-hundred chance at getting $100 (even though the expected value is just the same) gives one no more than a hope and an occasion to keep one's fingers crossed. So there are problems here.

3. The Problem of Adequacy

To be sure, probabilistic allocation is a process by which we in fact often proceed. The princess promised by her father to whoever solved a riddle could hardly be expected to divide her time equally between both of two suitably clever contestants. Again, when Hawaii became a state of the Union it had the opportunity afforded to all states of electing two senators. However, under the constitution one of these was to be junior senator with a three-year term and the other to be senior senator with a term of six years. The claims of the two new senators were equal but one of them had to be awarded an advantage over the other. For the sake of fairness, the issue was settled by a coin toss that gave each party an equality of mathematical expectation.

And so in a wide range of cases it is sensible to use mathematical expectation as a general guideline for a judicially reasonable decision. But are Leibniz and Keynes indeed right in claiming that it is *always* suitable? The fact is that complications lurk beneath the surface here.

For one thing, the presence of uncertainty will cause problems where fairness comes upon the scene. For as we saw in chapter 2, strict fairness requires a qualitative as well as a quantitative partitioning. Thus suppose that someone dies leaving his two cousins to share his estate consisting of $100 cash and a $100,000 lottery ticket with a one-in-a-thousand chance of winning. The (expected) value of that lottery ticket is clearly also $100. But it would not be fair to give $100 to one claimant and the lottery ticket to the other. For this allocation grants the one a sure thing and merely allocates a contingency to the other. The fair thing is clearly to give each both $50 and a half-interest in that lottery ticket. Giving or receiving the same expectation is just not tantamount to giving or receiving one's fair share. To give someone a *chance* of obtaining some good—essentially to let them have a lottery ticket—is just not the same as giving them a fixed share of this good, even though the expected value of these two alternatives may be exactly the same. We can certainly price out probabilistically contingent allocations in terms of expected values. But from the standpoint of the objective pricing of goods that is inherent in the concept of fairness, those probabilistically contingent values are never altogether equivalent to concrete assets.

The trouble with the expected-value approach of Leibniz and Keynes is that it rushes the recourse to probabilities. As emerged in the deliberations of chapter 2, probabilistic distributions enter into a just allocation process only late in the game—at the very end of the line, so to speak. To view them as an appropriate vehicle of share determination in general—from the outset as readily as from the end—is simply a violation of due process in the context.

The probabilistic expected-value assessment of claims also confronts still deeper difficulties whose exploration requires a chapter unto itself.[13]

Notes

1. Leibniz refers to him as "the famous jurisconsult (*ictus*) of Hamburg, whose learning, industry, and profundity and unusually good intentions I esteem highly." Letter of Gabriel Wagner of late 1696 (*Philosophische Schriften*, edited by C. I. Gerhardt, Vol. VII (Berlin: Weidmann, 1890), p. 518.
2. Leibniz's Latin letter is printed in his *Opera omnia*, edited by Ludovico Dutens (Geneva, 1768); see vol. VI, pt. 1, p. 36. It is quoted in Keynes 1921, p. 311.
3. Note that Leibniz does not, however, think that expected values are inevitably a decisive guide to assessing the acceptability of gambles. "Un homme qui a 20 000 écus de bein, ne doit pas le hazarder en un seul coup contre 100 000 écus, car ces 100 000 gagnés n'augmenteront pas beaucoup son bonheur, et les 20 000 perdus le rendront misérable" (*Opuscules et fragments inédits de Leibniz*, ed., Louis Couturat [Paris: Alcan, 1903], pp. 182-83). This line of thought prefigures the distinction between mathematical and moral expectation underpinning David Bernoulli's 1738 proposal for resolving the St. Petersburg Paradox. And it accordingly anticipates D'Alembert's question that, given the choice between a .99 probability of 1,000 écus and a .01 probability of 99,000 écus, "where is the man so foolish as to prefer the offer of 99,000 écus? The *expectation* in the two cases is not *really* the same; even though it is the same according to the results of probability" (*Oevres mathématiques* [Paris, 1761-80], vol. 4, p. 83). Cf. also the discussion of this issue in the authors *Risk: A Philosophical Introduction to the Theory of Risk Evaluation and Management* (Washington, DC: University Press of America, 1983), pp. 70-76.
4. Though a professional lawyer, Leibniz, like Pascal, sought to get at fair contracts via probability, while Huygen and DeWitt wanted to do it the other way around. See the interesting analysis in Lorrain Daston, *Classical Probability in the Enlightenment*, (Princeton, NJ: Princeton University Press, 1968), pp. 28-9 and passim.
5. G. W. Leibniz, *New Essays*, Bk. IV, chap. XVI, sec. 9; Academy edition, pp. 465-66.
6. J. M. Keynes, *A Treatise on Probability* (London: Macmillan, 1921), p. 311.
7. Couturat, *Opuscules*, pp. 569-70.
8. Si ex omnibus eventibus aliquot dent rem A, aliquote alii rem B, et reliqui rem C, erit spes tota aggregatum es rebus singulis in numerum eventuum qui eas dare possunt ductis, divisum per numerum eventuum possibilium omnium. Ut si numerus

eventuum qui dare possunt rem A sit a, numerus eventuum qui dare possunt rem B sit b, et numerus eventuum qui dare possunt rem C sit c, et numerus omnium eventuum sit n, erit spes

$$s \text{ aequ } \frac{aA + bB + cC}{n}$$

The connection between hope (*spes*, expectation) and probability goes back to Locke: "Hope is that pleasure in the mind, which everyone finds himself, upon the thought of a probable future enjoyment of a thing which is apt to delight him" (*Essays Concerning Human Understanding*, Bk. II, chap. 20).

9. Couturat, *Opuscules*, p. 226; cp. *New Essays*, Bk. IV, chap. XVI, sec. 9; Academy edition, p. 465.
10. Leibniz, *New Essays*, Bk. IV, chap. II, sec. 14; Academy edition, p. 372. Again:
    Bona malave aestimanda sunt separatim tum ex magnitudine sua, tum ex probabilitate. . . . Et, si aequalia sint erunt in ratione probabilitatis, si aeque probabilia, in ratione magnitudinis. Et si inaequalia et inaequaliter probabilia sint, erunt in ratione composita magnitudinis et probabilitatis (G. W. Leibniz, *Vorausedition*, Faszikel 6 [Muenster: Leibniz-Forschungsstelle, 1987], pp. 1136-1137).
11. Leibniz, *New Essays*, Bk. II, chap. XXI, sec. 66, Academy edition, pp. 205-206.
12. J. M. Keynes, *A Treatise on Probability*, p. 311, n. 1. More recently, John Broome has also argued that when people have unequal claims to a scarce, indivisible good, fairness requires that it be divided among them probabilistically, with the probability of an individual's receiving it adjusted to the proportional strength of his or her claim. See Elster 1988, p. 170.
13. This chapter's account of the historical background draws upon Rescher 1989.

6

Predominantism:
Limits of Proportionism in Pre-Ownership

(1) Rival claims can be resolved on the basis of proportionism ("Attune shares to claims") or predominantism ("Treat the strongest claims as decisive"). The former is appropriate in cases of ownership creation, but in the cases of ownership recognition the latter is appropriate. (2) On this issue the medieval Talmudists took the appropriate and correct view in opting for legal predominantism. (3) And so the Leibniz-Keynes doctrine of the pervasive appropriateness of expected value resolutions seems to go awry. (4) However, the rationale of predominantism in ownership cases itself rests on considerations of probabilistic expectation. (6) The upshot is that Leibniz-Keynes doctrine of a distributive probabilism based on mathematical expectations can itself be rationalized probabilistically at the deeper level of validating considerations.

1. Proportionalism vs. Predominance

Two very different approaches to distributive justice in the face of competing claims can plausibly be contemplated: the one based on proportionality, the other on predominance. The former, proportionalism, aligns shares to the magnitude of claims, while the latter, predominantism, proceeds by decisively "tipping the balance" in favor of the greatest claim with that side prevailing all out whose claim has comparatively the heaviest weight, by however little (see sect. 2 of chapter 2).

Traditional legal practice firmly opts for this second, leader-takes-all predominantist approach when it comes to dividing contested property. Virtually every legal system proceeds by determining the strongest claim and making its award of contested property strictly on this basis, setting the claims of the lesser claimants at nought.[1] In view of this situation, it is not surprising to find Keynes conceding, as we have seen, that the proportionist approach, which he joins

Leibniz in favoring, is such that "I am not aware that it has ever been acted on."[2] In matters of contested ownership, established legal practice is everywhere squarely on the side of predominantism. To be sure, this circumstance of widespread currency does not of itself settle the issue of whether this approach is reasonable, just, and proper. And so, the question remains: does the deeper justice of the matter lie with Leibniz and Keynes in their advocacy of expected-value proportionism?

A strong case can, in fact, be made against Leibniz and Keynes and in favor of the traditional predominantist approach in legal cases of contested ownership. But to see this, it is necessary to distinguish clearly between two importantly different sorts of distributive allocation situations, namely that of ownership *creation* in allocating heretofore unowned assets, and that of ownership *determination* in a situation of evidential insufficiency (uncertainty) concerning pre-existing ownership. The former is a matter of *competing ENTITLEMENT considerations for allocation in a no-ownership situation.* The latter is a matter of the *adjudication of conflicting EVIDENTIAL considerations in a situation where an ownership relation is already present.* Two very different things are at issue here, namely claims to *new-ownership inauguration* in the one case and claims to *pre-ownership recognition* in the other. Let us examine more closely what is at issue here.

The issue of *ownership creation* is typified by the historic problem of dividing the stake when a dicing game must be prematurely terminated—exactly the sort of issue that initially gave rise to the calculus of probability. In such cases of game-interruption, there is yet no ownership of the "pot"—there are simply variable claims, entitlement-consideration of variable strength. The division that is being made is designed to initiate possession and create ownership. The controlling factor with ownership inauguration is simply that of fairness to the competitors. An analogous legal example might be that of a wealthy decedent who has died leaving his estate to his domestic servants in otherwise unspecified proportions subject to the indefinite specification that it is "to be distributed according to service." It transpires that these beneficiaries have differential claims, some having many years service, others having recently joined the staff, some being minor functionaries while others carried substantial responsibility. Exactly as with the gambling case, every party here has some claim on assets that no one as yet actually owns. In this sort of situation, a proportional division by strength of claim—say on the basis of length and manner of service—seems perfectly equitable, exactly because it treats everyone alike in allocating to each contesting party a share proportionate to the strength of its particular case. The pivotal point is that where there are as yet no pre-established ownership rights upon the scene, but only a plurality of competing claims to be accommodated, it seems altogether just, proper, and reasonable to effect a proportionate division in line with the respective strength of these variable claims.

However, a very different sort of situation arises where a proprietary interest already exists, but there merely is *evidential uncertainty* regarding the identity of the actual owner. Take for example the situation when two different John Smiths claim a lost-and-found item known to belong to a John Smith who is bound to be one or the other of them. Or again, take Leibniz's own example of there being some question about which of two parties it is to whom a tract of land has been conveyed in some transaction. In all such cases, the actual practice in legal systems of every sort is to recognize the ownership of the party whose case is the strongest. And this approach is standard in many other contexts as well—for example with allocating credit for geographic or scientific discoveries (as in the dispute of Peary vs. Cook as claimants to the discovery of the North Pole). Our concept of just allocation operates in such a way that we standardly treat all such cases as a form of existing ownership and so not divide the credit claim-proportionately but follow the rule that the strongest claim prevails.

Again, take the case of King Solomon and the baby being contested between two rival "mothers." Solomon ingeniously begins by proposing a physical division: cutting the baby in two. But this should be regarded as simply a ruse to find out who the real mother actually is, and with this end achieved the wise king's award was made routinely on this basis.

Cicero, and the Roman jurists generally, adopted the dictum that justice consists in "giving to each his own" *(suum cuique tribuens)*.[3] But with a distribution of as yet unowned goods, the individual by hypothesis *owns* nothing; at the most, the thing he "has" is *a claim* (or perhaps *an obligation* when negativities rather than positivities are being distributed). But where there is actual ownership this fact becomes the paramount consideration in the eyes of justice.[4]

It is suggestive in this regard to revisit the Aristotelian distinction between *distributive* and *corrective* justice.[5] In the context of the present deliberations it seems sensible to reconstrue the former as properly concerning itself with the distributional division of heretofore unallocated assets held as common property, and the latter as not concerned with *distribution* at all, but with the *restoration* of a *status quo ante* in situations of pre-existing ownership. And very different principles will be operative here. For in cases of the accommodation of the claims at issue with no-ownership situations, distributive proportionalism makes eminent sense. But in cases where a situation of ownership is already in place as a somehow accomplished antecedent fact, it can be seen that proportionalism is ethically inappropriate. Here one has to do the best one can to accommodate that accomplished fact and predominantism is therefore the appropriate policy.

To be sure, the preceding case for predominantism lies open to an interesting objection that runs as follows:

> The proposed account endorses the justice of using the rule of claim dominance for established ownership cases and the rule of claim proportionality for ownership establishment cases. But suppose a situation where only one organ is available for transplantation to one of two potential recipients. And let it be that while other things are equal, one of them has a life expectancy of 10 years and the other of 20. Here, clearly, there is a no-ownership situation, so that a claim proportionality is called for on the proposed approach. And since we are dealing with an indivisible and unshareable good, this would have to be implemented probabilistically, presumably on the basis of a two-to-one ratio, with claim establishment through life-expectancy considerations. And yet it seems intuitively clear that the appropriate thing to do is to proceed by claim dominance, dedicating the organ outright to the recipient whose life expectancy is substantially longer. But this is diametrically opposed to the suggested analysis.[6]

The appropriate response to this seemingly plausible objection lies in seeing the case at issue as one of a *conflict of desiderata*. For abstract justice indeed requires the fairness of claim-proportionality with its probabilistic implementation in cases of an indivisible dividendum. But, on the other hand, utilitarian considerations of the efficienty allocation of a scarce resource call for proceeding by claim dominance. These conflicting desiderata must be weighed off against each other and balanced out. And here the claims of social utility appear to override those of a rigoristically justice-oriented proportionality. After all, fairness is only one desideratum among others, and in some cases it can plausibly be overridden by broader considerations of social advantage.

As this perspective indicates, the claims of abstract justice to individuals and that of social advantage and the general good can come into collision. The situation is analogous to that which arises when people with minor physical disabilities are exempted from the military draft. In justice they should stand at equal risk, but considerations of public policy militate against this. After all, we frequently depart from the principle *fact justitia ruat caelum* where substantial public interests are involved. (Why else plea bargaining?)

This perspective makes it possible to combine the present position regarding the call of rigorous justice with a concession that in exceptional circumstances a departure from its demands might be in order. Such cases must, of course, be seen as exceptional, and lest disaster ensue, they must be both rare and substantially justified. (One does not have to be a close student of the French Revolution to appreciate that few principles of public policy are more dangerous when carried to extremes than that of letting "the general good" systematically override the claims of individual justice.)

2. A Historical Interlude

Interestingly, the matter of ownership creation versus recognition was viewed in exactly the right perspective by those masters of legalistic subtlety, the medieval Talmudists. For consider:

> The Talmud tells of a man who learned that of the ten sons his wife bore, he was the father of only one. Before his death, he bequeathed his entire estate to his only son, without specifying who he was. The case came before Rabbi Bana'ah who instructed the ten claimants. "Go beat on your father's grave until he will arise and reveal to you to whom he left his [property]" (*Bava Batra*, 58a). Only one of the sons refrained from such disrespectful behavior, and so Rabbi Bana'ah awarded the bequest to him. Rabbi Asher in the course of a responsum dealing with verdicts based on probabilities comments: On the strength of this ... we do not say 'Let it stay till Elijah comes' [that is—let judgement be suspended and the property be held in escrow by the court]; rather let him judge in accordance with what his eyes behold, a probable opinion. On a small probability—that it appeared to him that the true son had respect for his father firmly implanted in his heart and paid him honor—he gave him all the property" [Rabbi Asher ben Yehiel, *Responsa* 107:6 (p. 196, col. 2)].

Here we have a case where as far as surface appearances go all the claims are initially of equal probability. The test devised to ascertain who is the true son is certainly not an unproblematically decisive one: Rabbi Asher emphasizes that it is only a "small probability." Yet because one claim has a higher probability than any of the others, we are justified in reaching a decision:

96   Fairness

> It ought to be pointed out that this case is quite unlike that discussed above . . . [when a husband and wife were both killed in the collapse of a house, the question arose whether his or her heirs are to inherit in the face of a contention about who died first] where the ruling is that the "property that is in doubt is to be divided equally." The Talmud distinguishes between a dispute where all the conflicting ownership claims have equal probability but only one has true validity, and a case in which all claims may in fact be equally valid, so that an equal division may well be in order. In the latter case, equal division is indicated, but in the former, since the entire property really belongs to one claimant only, if the evidence is equally balanced, no verdict can be rendered and the property must be held in escrow "till Elijah comes" (*Bara Metza*, 3a).[7]

The acute rabbis got the matter exactly right. On the one hand, in the case of the two conflicting groups of heirs contesting a legacy, there is no pre-existingly valid fact of ownership, and a proportional division is perfectly right and proper. On the other hand, in the case of the unidentified son, the problem is one of acknowledging the claims of the one and only valid heir, and an allocation in line with the single maxiprobable claim is quite in order. The rabbinic analysis is right on target in its differential approach to cases of pre-existing claims as contrasted with cases of claim creation.

However, another division problem arising in a no-ownership situation that was treated by the ancient rabbis is far more puzzling. It comes from the second century AD, from the Babylonian Talmud (Mishna) and runs as follows. Suppose that a man dies owing three claimants, say A, B, and C, debts of 100, 200, and 300 zuz, respectively. His estate comes to 300 zuz, total. And the rabbinic stipulation then is that A is to get one-sixth, B on third, and C one half of this sum, for a total of 50, 100, and 150 zuz respectively. Each receives a share amounting to one half of his claim in proportion with the available funds. So far so good. Most modern legal proceedings in estate or bankruptcy matters would issue in the same result. But now comes something odd. For the Talmud goes on to stipulate that if the estate were 200 zuz A is to receive 50 and B and C equal shares of 75, despite the inequality of their claims. And if the estate were 100 then all three are to receive an equal one-third, that is 33 1/3 zuz.[8]

It is perhaps difficult but certainly not impossible to make smooth sense of this position. For to all appearances its rationale appears to be a *mixture* of proportionalism and equality. The idea seems to be that proportionalism can be afforded up to a point, and that then equality take over. The operative rules at work here seem to be something like this:

I. As long as the estate does not fall below one-half of the overall claims, divide it by proportionately.

II. After this point is reached, continue to keep the minimal recipient(s) at the preceding (one-half proportionate) level and divide the rest of the estate equally among the remaining claimants—UNLESS

III. Following this rule plunges one of the more comparatively deserving claimants beneath the level of the minimal claimant. Once this point is reached, the estate is to be divided equally among *all* the claimants.

The pivotal factor here seems to be one half: half of the estate, and half of the minimum. And the grounding idea seems to be that *in extremis*—when the estate falls beneath the half-the-claim level—a transition from share proportionality to share equalization should be instituted step by step.

On this basis, the division would be:

		Size of the Estate				
		600	300	200	150	100
Size	A	100	50	50	50	$33\frac{1}{3}$
of	B	200	100	75	50	$33\frac{1}{3}$
Shares	C	300	150	75	50	$33\frac{1}{3}$

Here, proportionism and equality seem to collaborate as operative principles: with a mixture of the two coming into play with estates of a size intermediate between minimal adequacy and outright insufficiency. On this basis, it would appear that no new and exotic principles of division need be invoked to accommodate this somewhat eccentric example.

3. Leibniz and Keynes at Sea?

As this perspective on the matter indicates, the error committed by Leibniz—and also by Keynes in endorsing his probabilistic proportionalism as unqualifiedly "sensible" to the exclusion of predominantism—lies in assimilating the case of ownership *determination* at issue in situations of Aristotelian corrective justice to that of ownership *creation* at issue in situations of Aristotelian distributive justice. With ownership inauguration or *creation*, the proportionalist approach is altogether right and proper, in acknowledging the variable strength that competing claims exert on an ownership-indeterminate situation. For when a division is to be made in the absence of any pre-existing ownership entitlements, proportionality by claims does least violence to the principles of justice so that fairness is the order of the day.

However, with ownership *determination* the matter stands on a very different footing. Here, any sort of proportional division (be it by partition into shares or by a probabilistic allocation—however "fair"-seeming) has the defect of treating all claimants uniformly in a situation that is not uniform since by hypothesis one of them, unlike the others, is actually the owner of the contested item. In such situations of pre-existing ownership, the salient issue is not so much fairness as one of a rigorously corrective justice that must give ownership entitlements their due; in simple justice they be brushed aside as an irrelevant inconvenience. For here, as we have seen, the interests of justice are best served by a predominantism that acknowledges the strongest claimant as proper owner.[9]

And there is good reason for this in a larger perspective. For from the angle of social policy, the ideal of awarding a pre-owned but contested item by a claim-proportionate lottery has the important disadvantage of creating extensive insecurity and uncertainty of tenure. If there is a real (albeit small) chance that a remotely plausible claim could take a family farm or business away from a tenant otherwise in (relatively) secure possession, this would divert capital away from improving and extending such an enterprise into *insuring* it. Here pragmatism and justice stand in accord.

4. Why Predominantism in Ownership Cases

And so the lesson emerges that proportionalism ("attune shares to claims") is appropriate in cases of ownership *creation*, whereas predominantism ("Treat the largest claims as decisive") is the appropriate policy in cases of ownership *recognition*. And there is good reason for this.

To get a clear view of the rationale for taking the predominantist, leader-takes-all approach consider the following sort of situation:

> Let it be that there is an item of substantial value V whose possession is contested between two parties, A and B, in circumstances where no one else has any plausible claim to this item. And let it be that, relative to the evidence at hand, the case for crediting this item to A is somewhat stronger than the case for crediting it to B. Then how, by rights, should the total value V be divided between A and B?

Suppose that we divide the contested value between A and B in the proportion $x: (1 - x)$ for some as yet undecided value where $0 \leq x \leq 1$. Now, if the item in contention actually belongs to A, then its owner has been short-changed by the quantity $1 - x$. On the other hand, if it actually belongs to B, then its owner has been short-changed by the quantity x. Let us further specify:

p = the probability that the contested item actually belongs to A

$1 - p$ = the probability that the contested item actually belongs to B

(Note the by assumption $p > 1/2$.) On this basis, we can now calculate the overall expectation of short-changing the true owner of the item under contention:

$$p(1-x) + (1-p)x = p - 2px + x = p + x(1 - 2p).$$

Since $1 - 2p$ is *ex hypothesi* negative, the expectation at issue is clearly minimized (to $1 - p$) by setting $x = 1$. Here proportionate allocation unquestionably *increases* the prospect of an injustice. The predominantist leader-take-all method is demonstrably preferable in contexts of contested ownership: it maximizes the likelihood of doing the just and proper thing.

It is also helpful to consider the matter in a somewhat different perspective. Suppose that in a case of the preceding sort we were to allocate the item to A or B *probabilistically* (by lottery of the like) with

q = pr (the award goes to A)
$1 - q$ = pr (the award goes to B).

Then an injustice occurs when we award the contested item to A where it actually belongs to B or again when we award it to B where it actually belongs to A. Since we may assume that the probabilities involved are independent, the overall probability of an *injustice* is:

$$q(1 - p) + (1 - q)p = p + q - 2pq = p + q(1 - 2p).$$

Since $1 - 2p$ is negative (because by hypothesis $p >$), we minimize this quantity with $q = 1$. From this perspective too, it emerges that we must make our allocation all out in line with the stronger claim to minimize the likelihood of injustice. (The proportional allocation effected by letting $q = p$ certainly does *not* fill the bill.)

One recent theorist declares: "If claims of equal strength should receive equal treatment then it is implausible that a slightly stronger claim should totally override a slightly weaker one."[10] But if the present discussion holds this is very much an oversimplification because the issue depends critically on whether these claims are claims to ownership-acknowledgement or claims to ownership-creation. For as the preceding considerations indicate, with ownership *determination* (rather than ownership *inauguration*) the justice-inherent desideratum of minimizing the expectation of short-changing the proper owner requires the leader-takes-all methodology reflected in the traditional legal approach. Proceeding by proportionality in cases of pre-existing ownership involves the two-sided injustice in giving the rightful owner less than his just due and the other parties more.

An important principle lies in the background here. The failure of proportionality to meet the demands of justice in situations of pre-existing ownership is clear and intuitive. If a group jointly finds a long-buried treasure, it is only fair that they should all share such a treasure-trove alike. But if the "find" is something that actually already belongs to one of them in having been lost a matter of days or months ago, then that is clearly where it should go. Once ownership is an established fact—once there has been some act or transaction that gives somebody a valid claim to ownership—then justice requires us to do the very best we can to acknowledge this circumstance.[11] As far as the rights and wrongs of the matter go, established ownership makes a decisive difference.

The lesson is clear. When preestablished ownership is at issue, what is called for is not proportionalized fairness among causal claimants but justice by way of a predominantism that favors the owner. After all, the object here is not justifiable division but restitution, and corrective justice.[12]

It deserves incidental note that an interesting application of the same general principle arises in the epistemic setting of the rational allocation of credence. Statements have a claim to acceptance based on the extent to which the evidence supports them in terms of the quantity and quality of the substantiating considerations that it affords. In matters of inquiry it is clearly preponderance that counts: When we have questions and need to have them answered that proposition deserves acceptance as the best available answer to our questions which has the strongest evidence in its favor. Here the strongest arguments deserve to prevail; to proceed probabilistically would be "unfair"—or, rather, in the present case *unreasonable*. The case is really one of ownership: Reality, so to speak, owns the true answers to our questions.

5. The Lesson

The upshot of these deliberations is relatively straightforward. In assimilating the situation of an ownership dispute at law to the quite different situation of dividing the stake in games of chance, Leibniz and Keynes succumbed to a misleading oversight. With ownership creation in the division of gaming stakes the proportionality principle is in general patently sensible and just. But with claims in matters of established ownership, proportionality is inappropriate and violates the demands of distributive justice. Their enthusiasm for the expected-value approach carried these two eminent theorists too far into endorsing proportionalism based on expected values as an allocation mechanism even in situations where this is nowise appropriate.

But now observe a significant and noteworthy circumstance. Those arguments that were deployed above to establish the inappropriateness of the expected-value standard of proportionate shares in this contested-ownership case themselves turn on use of an expected-value assessment, proceeding by means of expected-value comparisons in their resort to minimizing the expectation of shortchanging people and making unjust awards. Interestingly, the inappropriateness of allocation by particular expectations is a fact that itself comes to light by means of larger, more fundamental expected-value considerations.

In the end, then, such an analysis reinforces rather than impairs the Leibniz-Keynes doctrine of the utility of expected values as standards of rational appraisal in matters of distributive justice. For here too proportionism prevails once more at the deeper level of justifactory considerations.[13]

Notes

1. A rather extreme (and, as our subsequent analysis will show, very questionable) example of this is afforded by the famous case of Summers v. Tice, 33 Cal.2d 80, 199 P.2d 1 (1948), where two defendants shot at a plaintiff with equal likelihood that each person's shot proved fatal. The court held that the loss was joint and several, so that each defendant was liable for the whole, but had an action against the other for 50 percent contribution, if he were solvent. If it could have been known that one defendant had a greater chance of having fired the bullet, his would have been the total loss, notwithstanding the equal culpability of the other. The same result would hold if the defendant who shot the plaintiff was guilty only of ordinary negligence, while the one who missed had engaged in reckless conduct. See Richard A. Epstein, "Luck," *Social Philosophy and Policy*, vol. 6 (1988), p. 22.
2. Keynes 1921, p. 311, n 1.
3. Jesus' advice to "Render unto Caesar that which is Caesar's and unto God that which is God's" is a strict parallel.
4. To be sure our present discussion leaves aside the issue of how appropriate ownership claims are to be constituted.
5. Aristotle, *Nicomachean Ethics*, V, 2-4. (What is at issue in the following is not so much an *interpretation* of Aristotle's distinction of an *extension* of it.)
6. Regarding issues of this sort see Jon Elster, "Taming Chance: Randomization in Judicial and Social Decisions," The *Tanner Lectures on Human Values*, (Salt Lake City: University of Utah Press, 1988), pp. 105-89 (see p. 170), especially pp. 170-171.
7. Rabinovitz, 1973, pp. 127-28.
8. Brams and Taylor 1996 and Hill 2000.
9. The difference rests on a theoretical basis. With pre-established ownership, the missing information that prevents our making an ideally correct award relates to the accomplished past; with gambling division it relates to the contingent future. There being no fact of ownership here, we cannot see the available information as playing an evidential role.
10. Broome 1991, p. 196. It would seem that this author has never encountered a beam balance.
11. But what of the case where one does not *know* whether an ownership relation exists to warrant a property claim—say whether the ring found in a certain field was lost or thrown away by its owner. Then, the nature of the object would be determinative; with a ring it would be plausible to assume ownership, but if a nugget were found by the side of a stream in a gold-yielding region, it would be implausible to assume that a prospector had lost it there.
12. An early publication of the distributive justice theorist John Rawls was entitled "Justice as Fairness" (Rawls 1958). From the angle of the present deliberations the appropriateness of this motto becomes questionable in the absence of careful qualification.
13. Some of the ideas of this chapter are elaborated more fully in Rescher 1989.

7

Dividing Credit for Discoveries: Limits of Proportionalism in Teamwork

(1) Dividing credit for multi-participant discoveries requires distinguishing mere cooperation from actual collaboration or teamwork. (2) There is a big difference here as regards credit allocation because in the former case credit is divisible, in the latter not. (3) Nevertheless, the classic principle of a fair-shares proportionism can be maintained throughout. For with authentically collaborative teamwork there simply are no partitive and separately distributed claims. The two different modes of credit allocation find their respective rationales in the different goal structure of the two forms of investigative process.

1. Distributive vs. Collective Cooperation

The appropriateness of procedural principles in matters of distribution is bound to depend on the specific purposes at issue with the distribution. The allocation of credit for discoveries affords an illuminating case study in this regard.

How is credit for a discovery in science or elsewhere to be properly allocated where the conjoint effort of several individuals is involved? When a group of investigators cooperates in making a discovery, how should the credit for this achievement be apportioned among them to assure that everyone receives their proper share?

The problem being considered here is not that of assessing importance—of determining how much credit there is to go around.[1] That is something else again. The present problem, rather, is that of how that credit, be it great or small, should be allocated to the parties responsible for the discovery at issue? It is, once more, not the determination of credit but its distribution that is at issue.

In dealing with this question, an important preliminary must be addressed. There are two very different sorts of multilaterally cooperative investigations, since a multi-participant problem-solving effort can proceed either collectively or distributively. *Distributive cooperation* is simply coordinated effort towards the realization of a common goal, whereas actual *collaboration* or *collective cooperation* is a matter of teamwork, of working together conjointly towards such a goal with interactive feedback. (The term *cooperation* accordingly serves as a broader umbrella to cover both of these cases.)

Distributive problem solving occurs when the issues are disassembled into separate components that are addressed separately—often by distinct investigators—subject to a division of labor. Perhaps because variant specialties are at issue, each investigator (or investigative group) does its work separately and their efforts, though coordinated, are disjoint, with different contributors contributing different pieces of the whole. Thus with the lexicographic problem of explaining the etymology of English words we may have a research mode where investigator No. 1 may take on the *A*'s, investigator No. 2 the *B*'s, or the like. Again, in a cryptological effort one investigator might work on verbs and adverbs another on nouns and adjectives, another on particles, etc. Different investigators, that is to say, take on different constituent sub-problems of the whole: they are subcontractors, as it were, who contribute their separate parts to an overall effort.

However, a very different situation obtains when cooperative problem solving proceeds collaboratively. Here there is not just cooperation but actual teamwork with different investigators fusing their efforts in conjoint interaction. Collaborative work on a crossword puzzle is a good example. As anyone who has tried it knows, the feedback interaction that comes into play here renders this something far more effective than simply compiling the results of different individuals working separately. For problem solving proceeds interactively, with the efforts of the different contributors inextricably interwoven. And we shall suppose that with genuinely collaborative cooperation none of the individuals involved is dispensable in that the work of the others would yield the discovery at issue without this individual's contribution.[2]

There are, of course, some problems that cannot be factored into constituent pieces. Such systemic problems as, for example, explaining the origins of World War I must be handled as an indivisible unit: to achieve unified causal account it makes no sense to address the historical, political, colonial, social, military, naval, and economic aspects of the problem separately. By their very nature as such, these are holistic problems where multilateral cooperation must of necessity take the form of interactive teamwork.[3]

Obviously, what matters most with distributive credit for a discovery is actually making it. Consider a schematic example. Let us suppose that the situation before us is a search process for a particular problem-resolution that is emplaced within an overall solution space with the structure of a tic-tac-toe grid that maps out the range of possibilities:

1	2	3
4	5	6
7	8	9

And now imagine a situation where two investigators X and Y work in an independent but coordinated way. Investigator X locates the solution in the first row of the solution space, and Y locates it in the middle column. Between them they have now solved the problem by identifying 2 as the solution. Each has eliminated six possibilities and the work they have done accordingly is (so we may suppose) equally significant. Other things being equal, they will thus divide the credit 50:50.

But now assume that Y's work had, like X's, *also* simply located the solution in the first row. Then of course the problem would remain unresolved: there would have been no discovery to be credited. To be sure, the useful work done by X and Y yield some credit for each of them, namely credit for their respective (identical) finding. And note furthermore that X has done *nothing different*: as far as what X does is concerned, there is no discernible difference between the two cases. But there is now no question of credit for the discovery of a solution since just this is now something that is notably absent. This schematic little example is thus also instructive by rendering it transparently clear that what matters for collective discovery is not just individual achievement but the overall result. In cooperative cases, discovery itself, and the credit that goes with it, is a contextual feature that hinges on what others do. Whether or not there is discovery—and therefore whether or not any credit for discovery is due to those investigators—depends holistically on the overall relationship of their respective contributions.

2. Principles of Credit Allocation

Given these preliminary clarifications, the fundamental principles of credit allocation for discoveries are now readily discerned. They are principally two:

1. When a group finding stems from *distributive* cooperation (in which case it must, of course, address a factorable problem), then the individual contributors simply get the credit that goes with their proportionate piece (or pieces) of the problem. Here the whole is equal to the sum of its parts and the parts get evaluated separately as making up so much percentage of the whole. However—

2. When a group finding stems from *collective* cooperation, credit cannot be allocated differentially. It belongs to the group members indivisibly, collectively, and equally: they all share and share alike with respect to the aggregate outcome. They are, to speak in legal terminology, *tenants in common* of the discovery at issue.[4] In fact, it would be inappropriate here to distribute partial credit to the individual investigators because in the conditions ex-hypothesi at issue there is no practicable way of doing so. Credit for genuinely collaborative teamwork is effectively indivisible and belongs to the group-as-a-whole and to individuals only as members thereof.

For the sake of an instructive albeit schematic example, consider once more the search for a problem-resolution emplaced within an overall solution space that has the structure of a tic-tac-toe grid:

1	2	3
4	5	6
7	8	9

We may again suppose that the problem at issue is factorable and that our two investigators X and Y work separately. But now let it be that investigator X determines that the solution must lie on a diagonal, while investigator *Y* determines that it must lie in the middle row. Between the two they accordingly place it in the middle as solution 5. They have solved the problem and between the two they get credit for the whole. But each gets credit only for the particular piece—the particular sub-problem resolved by himself. And so, overall the credit is now divided as follows. *X* eliminates 4 possibilities (and thus 4/9 of the whole spectrum) while *Y* eliminates 6 possibilities (and thus 6/9 of the whole spectrum). Thus *Y* makes a contribution half again as large as *X*'s. (Of course this assumes that all else is equal, which is assuming a lot.)

With factorable problems credit is thus a matter of division or partition. The classic precept of distributive justice obtains: to each their due. Here the overall credit is fairly divided with shares proportionate to claims. With distributive contributions, the whole is equal to the sum of its parts: whatever credit there is will get shared out among the several individual contributors in line with their individual accomplishments.

With collective contributions, by contrast, where interactive teamwork is at stake, the credit cannot be divided. The group-as-a-whole will be the bearer of whatever credit there is. (In legal parlance, the contributors will own the credit in common and not by separable shares, the distinction being akin to that between a corporation and a partnership.)

Yet why not say that if there are *n*-interactive collaborators each simply gets one-*n*th of the credit? Because it makes no sense to so do. Participating with various others in teamwork leading to a great discovery is just not the same sort of thing as making one modest-size discovery on one's own. With genuine teamwork, credit for the collective achievement belongs substantially to the entire team—that is to everyone. To be sure, it is not that the discovery is to be credited *only* to the team and that individuals as such do not figure—that they deserve no personal recognition in the usual ways (raises, prizes, honorary degrees, etc.). It is, rather, that they deserve this as members of the team and that such good things should come to them all on a basis of equality ("all for one and one for all").[5] With teamwork credit belongs to the team as a whole and thereby to its individual members as members thereof: the credit is shared, but not divided.

But what of the *organizer* of a multilateral teamwork research effort? Does this prime mover not deserve a great deal of the credit?

Surely so. For what we usually have here is simply a divisible effort with one individual or group providing the planning and organization of the research and another group carrying out the work. This being so, the overall process of problem-solving is, in fact, divisible, being factorable into two sectors: organizing the collaboration and then conducting the inquiry. And then each party gets credit for its own contribution: the organizers for the organization of the inquiry, the implementers for the work of discovery. Neither party deserves credit for the contribution of the other: the organizers get a lion's share of credit for the conceptual design of the inquiry, and its organizational implementation, while the investigators get the cognitive credit for whatever accomplishments are achieved. (Consider an analogy: the statesmen and decision makers who arranged for sending Columbus or Lewis and Clark on their voyages of exploration deserve much credit for making discoveries possible, but credit for the discoveries themselves belongs to those who actually made them.). Of course, when the organizers also function as active investigators and are themselves members of the research team, then they deserve whatever additional credit goes with the discharge of this role.

In sum, then, with collective collaboration the credit for discovery will also have to be collective, while with distributive collaboration it will have to be distributive by shares. The mode of problem-solving collaboration dictates the mode of credit-allocation that is appropriate. And, in particular, while there may be much credit in the results of an inquiry that proceeds by way of the division of labor inherent in a distributive cooperation, nevertheless the contributors can here claim credit only for the particular finding that is their personal contribution.[6]

3. Fairness Sustained

With distributive collaborations, credit for discoveries is thus comparatively unproblematic since contributions can here be broken apart and credited to specific individuals. Accordingly, the classic principle of fair-share proportionalism obtains in this setting, with credit being divided in line with individual claims. However, with collective credit for solving nonfactorable problems the situation is more complex. Here there is no proportioning of shares. Nevertheless, the classic principle of proportionality/fairness is not actually violated. For *here there actually are no competing individual claims*. With collective collaboration, claims have to be made in the first instance on behalf of the group-as-a-whole and credit then allocated to individuals as members thereof. The claim of each individual participant is simply that of having functioned as an integral and essential member of the entire team. And the credit he gets is a matter of shining as a moon reflecting the bright sunlight of collective achievement.

Accordingly, it needs to be stressed that the special situation of teamwork in discovery does *not* violate the classic fairness/proportionality principle of traditional distributive justice that allocations be made in accordance with claims. And the reason for this lies in the way in which claims work in this domain—namely, that with authentically collaborative teamwork there simply are no partitive and separately distributed claims.

But how is this difference in the ground rules for credit allocation, as between distributive and collective collaboration (teamwork) to be explained. The rationale at issue is clearly functional and pragmatic. In cases of the division of labor we want to provide each party with the strongest possible incentive for doing their individual part competently and efficiently. And so it makes good sense to give them full credit for their own contribution and thereby not to let them any share in somebody else's. With teamwork, however, the interests of functional efficiency point in a different direction. Treating the team as an integral unit—with achievement and failure belonging to the whole—creates conditions where the coordinated efforts of the group are powerfully motivated in the pursuit of a shared objective. Effectiveness in working together is the crux so that here efficiency and effectiveness is maximized by giving that unifying goal priority over the particular individual contributions of the various collaborators. In sum, the difference in distributive procedure roots in the different goal structures of the respective modes of investigative procedure. The efficacy of different procedures in realizing different sorts of objectives is the key.

This state of affairs has important ramifications that deserve a chapter unto itself.

Notes

1. The question of assessing the importance of a discovery is, of course, an interesting one. It is addressed in the Larry Laudan, *Progress and Its Problems* (Berkeley: University of California Press). See also Alvin Goldman and Moshe Shaked, "An Economic Model of Scientific Activity and Truth Acquisition," *Philosophical Studies*, vol. 63 (1991), pp. 31-55 (reprinted in Goldman's *Liaisons* 1992), as well as David Hull *Science as a Process: An Evolutionary Account of the Social and Conceptual Development of Science* (Chicago: University of Chicago Press, 1988). The importance of a scientific discovery is in general a matter of its reverberations—of how extensively it leads scientists to change their minds about relevant issues.
2. The situation here is fundamentally analogous to physical collaboration along the lines "Tom and Bob and Ted carried the piano upstairs" (as contrasted with say, the three of them digging up the potato patch). On these issues see Massey 1976.
3. An informative treatment of cooperation in general, without, however, any specific reference to inquiry or research, in Tuomela 2000.
4. "The central characteristic of a tenancy in common is simply that such tenant is deemed to own by himself, with most of the attributes of independent ownership, a physically individual part of the entire parcel." (Thomas F. Bergin and Paul G. Haskell, *Preface to Estates in Land and Future Interests*, 2nd ed., *University Textbook Series* [Foundation Press, 1991], p. 54)
5. Of course even within the setting of teamwork there are often subordinate inquires that can be factored out into subordinate inquiries for distributive pursuit. And some team members will generally deserve special credit on this basis. Thus one can often say that certain core contributions were due to one particular team member, which others then developed and refined in interactive fashion.
6. With papers publishing research findings produced under conditions of multilateral *distributive* cooperation it makes sense to list the names of the contributors in order of decreasing shares. With those produced under conditions of multilateral *collective* cooperation an alphabetical or anti-alphabetical order should ideally be used standardly and systematically to signalize the character of the inquiry.

8

The Pragmatic Rationale of Distribution Principles

(1) Allocations of epistemic and moral credit operate on very different principles seeing that moral praise and blame always appertains to individuals, never to collectives. Moreover, with moral credit intention is paramount and inadvertence is credit-annihilative. But with epistemic credit the matter is quite different in both these respects. (2) These differences inhere in the distinct goal-structures or teleology of the moral and epistemic projects. (3) The law also manifests characteristically distinctive features in its modus operandi *of allocating blame and punishment. (4) The matters of appropriate allocation principles is thus highly context dependent. (5) And the reason for such differences is ultimately pragmatic: their validating rationale pivots on the differential requisites for achieving efficacy and effectiveness in realizing the characteristic aims and purposes of the sort of distribution that is at issue.*

1. Epistemic vs. Moral Credit/Discredit

The appropriateness of principles governing credit allocation for cooperative discoveries may seem straightforward. Nevertheless, in particular cases this is something that can readily become quite complex. For example, consider the by-now familiar illustration of a problem-resolution space with the configuration of a tic-tac-toe grid:

1	2	3
4	5	6
7	8	9

We again suppose that there are two investigators X and Y working separately in noncollaborative cooperation. And now let it be that X

manages to determine that the solution lies in column three. But Y cheats. He purports to have shown that the solution must lie in regions 2 or 3, whereas actually all that he is entitled to claim on the basis of his findings is that it lies somewhere in the first row.

Note that:

1. Between the two of them they have solved the problem: as a group they get full marks.

2. By hypothesis, each has succeeded in eliminating six possibilities. And so as far as individual epistemic credit goes, their shares are equal.

3. However, as regards ethical or moral credit, the inquiry as a whole is contaminated by Y's cheating.

4. Nevertheless, from the ethical point of view X is altogether blameless: he is innocent as the driven snow. And so—

5. Y must bear the entire burden of ethical discredit.

6. However, Y's moral culpability and cheating nowise unravels the problem resolution collaboratively arrived at. Nor does it even abolish Y's *epistemic* credit for his contribution.

The example accordingly has some instructive ramifications. In particular, it brings to light the very different modus operandi of moral and epistemic credit. The two types of credit actually function in very different ways. And this crucial circumstance explains a great deal.

For one thing, it is an instructive and important feature of the theory of distributive justice that the difference between the goal-structure of the cognitive and of the moral enterprises provides the rationale—the explanatory basis—for the difference in the principles of credit allocation operative in these two domains. Thus consider:

1. *Moral credit is always individual; epistemic credit need not be so, for while it is also individualized with distributive co-operation, it is collectivized and indivisible with teamwork.*

Epistemic credit can belong to a group holistically and resist a distributive breakdown to individuals. But in matters of moral credit (or discredit) individuals stand on their own feet. Strictly speaking, there is no group credit/discredit in moral contexts: here the credit/discredit of groups is always that of the individuals who belong. And the rationale of this difference is straightforward.

With the *interactive collaboration* at issue in investigative teamwork, it makes sense to sink individual self-preoccupation in the interests of cooperation towards the common goal. And so from the angle of investigative teamwork there is good reason for establishing a strong disincentive to the idea "I'll do my separate bit and will keep my separate share, thank you." However, in moral matters individual action and inaction are the crux. So here, where *individual effort* is paramount, it is advantageous to maximize personal incentives. With individual responsibility credit must be treated on a strictly personal, individualized basis.

2. *With moral credit, intention is paramount but with epistemic credit intention is immaterial since results are paramount.*

It is not just that with moral credit or discredit intentions count but from the moral point of view, intent is critical. The wicked nephew poisons rich Aunt Agatha's tea. In the last moment the clumsy chambermaid knocks it over, and a fresh, harmless cup of tea is produced in its place. Legally the nephew is, of course, guiltless, but morally he is guilty as sin. The drowning child cries for help. You plunge into the raging waters to save him. When you are on the verge of taking hold of the infant, a great wave comes along and sweeps you both onto the shore. Your brave and selfless actions had no effect. But from the moral point of view you are still a hero. As such illustrations show, outcome is generally subordinate to intent plus effort from the angle of moral appraisal.[1]

But with epistemic credit the matter stands otherwise. Where discovery is concerned, results are all and good intentions and valiant but unavailing efforts count for nothing. And the rationale is again straightforward. In the moral case, where what matters is canalizing the smooth interaction of individuals in the promotion of the common interest, we put paramount emphasis on process—on how an individual proceeds in making decisions about courses of action, and therefore on motivation with respect to goals and intention. But in the epistemic case product is paramount: here results matter and intentions are irrelevant.

Moreover, this difference in process/product prioritization is also reflected in the following principle:

3. *In moral contexts, inadvertance is credit-annihilative but with epistemic credit serendipity counts.*

Doing the right thing unwittingly and by accident, gains you little if any moral credit, though as far as moral blame goes, this sort of thing helps to serve as exculpation. But things stand otherwise with epistemic credit. Accidental discoveries are still discoveries and deserve full marks as such.

Here, the difference once again, clearly lies in the fact that with moral credit process is paramount, while with epistemic credit results and hence product is paramount. In moral contexts we want to insist that people proceed reflectively and keep mindful of the rules so that individual action is the crux, while with teamwork in discovery it is the internalism of individuals that matters. The different aims of the two enterprises are once more determinative.

There is, moreover, another significant point of difference between the moral and the epistemic situation. In the case of collaborative discovery only a fixed amount of credit is available—namely the value of the discovery at issue—and the participants share it altogether. But in the case of moral right- or wrongdoing, in specific, there is no fixed amount of discredit to be shared by the group as a whole. All the individuals concerned stand on their own footing, and each culprit, severally and individually, becomes saddled with the whole of the reprehension at issue. Thus if two miscreants joint in deceiving or mistreating someone, each deserves blame for the whole of the misdeed: they do not divide it between them, nor would they each get half as much blame if there were twice as many malefactors. And the same holds for morally creditable actions as well.

In this sense, most credit and discredit is in fact fissionable. Consider wrongdoing. With collaborative theft or murder each participant is a thief or murderer—from the moral standpoint at least. And for good reason. The policy at issue is designed to serve as a maximally effective deterrent. Collective misdeeds redound upon all alike in the case of moral transgression even as collective achievements redound upon all alike in cases of collaborative discovery. In the latter case we seek to maximize the incentives to action that is appropriate and in the former to maximize the incentives against action that is inappropriate.

It is thus clear that, in general, markedly different policies and procedures are at issue with epistemic and moral credit. They have a different rationale, seeing that very different aims are at issue in the moral and the epistemic enterprises. With inquiry we want results: our epistemic concerns are result oriented—we want to advance the frontiers of knowledge. Product is paramount. Epistemic credit is achievement driven: the value of the findings that result is the decisive consideration. With morality, by contrast, we want good procedure: our moral concerns are process oriented—we want people to comport themselves properly and trust results to take care of themselves. Pragmatically or functionally different enterprises are at issue. Moral credit is process driven so that here what people *endeavor* to do is determinative.

Some significant lessons emerge from such comparisons: Epistemology and morality are both normative enterprises, but they differ sharply in point of teleology. Their functional or purposive dimension are markedly different, so that a very different rationale is operative with respect to credit allocation in these two cases. Moral credit pivots on process and intention; epistemic credit on product and accomplishments. And in consequence there arises a difference in distribution principle owing to the greater functional adequacy in point of effectiveness and efficiency in goal realization that these different principles are able to engender.

2. A Difference of Aims

This goal-oriented perspective brings to light the rationales for the allocation process at issue. Seen as a functional enterprise, the aim of morality lies in inculcating actions benefit of the wider safeguard the real interest of people through serving the best interest of the community. Morality thus seeks to canalize and direct the actions of all the people concerned through guiding and goading them into doing what is right by way of assuring the general interest of the group to the advantage of all concerned. Accordingly, the mission of the moral project is to promulgate and instill in people those modes of action that coinduce to the general advantage through protecting the interests of people-in-general in contexts of interaction. Morality accordingly spells out the rules—the do's and (primarily) don'ts heed of which will facilitate the shaping of a community where people are not inappropriately disadvantaged through the agency of others.

The crux is that process (what people do) is paramount for morality, with the issue of outcome (how things work out) as subsidiary and incidental since it lies largely outside the agent's control. In allocating moral credit and blame, praise or reprehension, intention thus become the pivotal factors—exactly as Kant emphasized long ago.

Of course the moral ideal is good results that issue from good intentions. But under sub-ideal conditions the principles for allocating moral credit or blame prioritize intent and outcome is left to take care of itself. Morality accordingly prioritizes effort as comparatively manageable and under our control. By contrast, outcome and all too often chancy and beyond our powers. Situations vary and outcomes are contingent and often lie outside the agent's effective control. People propose and the reality's course of events disposes. And it does so in all-too-often uncontrollable ways: outcome generally lies *extra vires*, beyond our power. However, intention and effort—with its emphasis on what we are *trying* to do—lies within the agent's control. Getting people to *try* to do the proper thing will generally optimize the chances of success. In sum, realizing the definitive goal of the moral enterprise is something that is better served by a policy that prioritizes intention and effort over outcome and performance.

By comparison, inquiry too is a functional enterprise. But it has a very different sort of goal-structure—one that prioritizes the achievement of knowledge. For the discomfort of unknowing is a natural component of human sensibility. To be ignorant of what goes on about us is almost physically painful for us—no doubt because it is so dangerous from an evolutionary point of view. It is a situational imperative for us humans to acquire information about the world. The requirement for information, for cognitive orientation within our environment, is as pressing a human need as that for food itself. The basic human urge to understand—to make sense of things—is an integral and characteristic aspect of our make-up—we cannot live a satisfying life in an environment we do not understand. For us intelligent creatures, cognitive orientation is itself a practical need: cognitive disorientation is physically stressful and distressing. And inquiry—the means by which we endeavor to satisfy this need—is accordingly product driven. The advancement of knowledge is the paramount task for the enterprise of inquiry. Here intent is irrelevant and achievement paramount.

As such a perspective shows, morality and inquiry are different enterprises with very different aims and purposes in view. And on this basis, it is not hard to see that the different allocation processes at issue with moral and epistemic credit inhere in a fundamentally *pragmatic* rationale. For it emerges that this difference in modus operandi can be explained on the basis of the efficiency and effectiveness of those different modes of credit allocation that facilitate realization of the definitive goals of these two distinct enterprises. After all, the rational legitimization of a practice or procedure or instrumentality lies in its effectiveness and efficiency at realizing the goals and purposes characteristic of the domain in which this practice or procedure or instrumentality has been instituted. Consider an example.

3. A Look at the Law

With the allocation of legal responsibility and culpability, we again come up against the fact that this enterprise has its own characteristic sort of goal structure. A comparison helps to illustrate this. Moral assessment pivots on what can reasonably be anticipated. People who drive their cars home from an office party in a thoroughly intoxicated condition, indifferent to the danger to themselves and heedless of the risks they are creating for others, are equally guilty in the eyes of *morality* (in contrast to *legality*) whether they kill someone along the way or not. Their transgression lies in the very fact of their playing Russian roulette with the lives of others. Whether they actually kill someone or not is simply a matter of chance, of accident and sheer statistical haphazard, of circumstances beyond their control, and therefore the moral negativity is much the same one way or the other—even as the moral positivity is much the same one way or the other for the person who bravely plunges into the water in an attempt to save a drowning child as the tide is drawing him out. Allocations of moral responsibility prioritize intentions. But legal responsibility works very differently. For allocations of legal responsibility prioritize outcome. If a drunk driver is lucky and does not kill someone his legal offense goes no further than drunk driving.

How is this difference between the moral and the legal situation to be accounted for? Very simply in functional terms. The difference roots in the difference of the different teleology—the different aims and purposes—of the enterprises concerned. For the project of morality and the project of legality each has its own characteristic mission. And it is this functional, purposive, pragmatic difference that explains the difference in credit allocation.

Suppose X, Y, and Z collaborate on an armed bank robbery. X enters the premises and does the stick-up work, Y acts as lookout, and Z drives the get-away car. The bank guard resists and X shoots him dead. From the moral point of view, X alone is a murderer—moral culpability always goes to those who are directly or indirectly responsible for the negativity at issue. Causality is the crux here. But from the legal point of view all are guilty of murder: even those who did not actually figure in the chain of causation leading to that shot. (In sentencing individual intentions may be taken into account, but it is thereby a second-order consideration.) With the law, the outcome of a cooperative crime takes the priority, because this will discourage people from cooperating in wrongdoing—or so the theory goes. The law accordingly prioritizes outcomes over individual intention in determining guilt or innocence. And the rationale for this difference, of course, lies in the paramount mission of the legal enterprise, namely, preserving the fabric of the social order that enables people-in-general to go about their affairs safe and secure in matters of life, limb, and property. So here too the *modus operandi* of credit and blame, reward and penalty has a rationale that lies in the functional nature of the enterprise.

4. Further Perspectives

It is instructive to consider an epistemological version of proportionalist fair division. The idea here is that of regarding credence in or acceptance of a proposition p as effectively constituting an allocation problem. There are two claimants here, the positive (+) and the negative (-), with the former insisting on acceptance and the latter on rejection. To which of these nominal claimants is the proposition p to be allocated? Each one stakes his claims by way of putting forward his overall case, pro and con respectively. How then is an allocation to be made?

Two epistemic postures now lie before us:

1. Predominantism/Evidentialism: Allocate the proposition to whatever side it is whose claims are strongest.
2. Proportionalism/Probabilism. Divide the proposition between the two rival claimants in proportion to the strength of their claims, in terms of the overall weight of the considerations that speak on its behalf.

In effect the former policy amounts to taking the line that rational-acceptability-as-true lies on the side of the stronger arguments. By contrast, the second policy rejects the idea of all-out acceptance or rejection and indeed assigns a weight of probability (or plausibility) that reflects the comparative strength of the case for (and/or against) accepting the proposition.

Both epistemic policies have had their adherents and supporters over the years. In the light of chapter 5's deliberations, it is clear where Leibniz's position lay: he can and should be seen as the founding father of a mode of probabilism that subsequently found its strongest supporters in the Keynes of the *Treatise on Probability* and the Rudolf Carnap of *The Foundations of Probability*. Other theorists reject such probabilism and insist that in epistemic context the strongest argument must prevail. There is no consensus among epistemologists here. And the reason is that this once again lies in the fact that *fundamentally different contexts* can be at issue. In practical contexts alone *action* is paramount and matters must be decided one way or the other, predominantism is clearly in order. But in purely theoretical matters where there is not need to "rush to judgment" probabilism is a sensible policy.

It is also instructive to consider a sociological analogue to proportionalist fair division: the problem of conflicting obligations that make claims upon a person. Thus consider someone who has the task of maintaining her commitments to her work, her family, her friends, as well as (obviously) herself. When she rates these (on a scale of 1-10) by urgency and importance the result may be something as follows:

	Rating	*Proportional Rating*
Family	10	10/28
Hobbies	6	6/28
Friends	6	6/28
Self-development	6	6/28
TOTAL	28	

Now, after allowing eight hours for sleeping, eight for working, two for eating, one for grooming, and one for transportation, there still remain four hours per diem for free disposal. With proportionate allocation this would in the present case yield (on average) roughly one and one-half hours for family time, and three quarter-hours each for hobbies, friends, and self-development.

This example has an obvious bearing on our present context. For it is clear that in such situations a claim-proportionate division would once again make good sense. Predominantism would clearly be absurd in the purposive context at issue. This sort of example further reinforces the need to acknowledge that the issue of the appropriateness of allocation principles is highly context-dependent with reference to the relevant teleology.

5. The Big Picture: Functionalistic Pragmatism

The thesis that this book has sought to defend and illustrate is that ethical considerations mandate that *when positivities or negativities are to be allocated, this should be done fairly*, that is, *proportionately with correlative claims*. To be sure, there are also cases where credit (or discredit) belongs holistically to the group-as-a-whole, inquiry by collaborative teamwork affording a preeminent example. Moreover, there are cases where division is not in order at all (for example, with penalties for crimes). But the paramount fact is that exactly the same underlying rationale is uniformly at work here. For throughout, it is the functional mission of the relevant enterprise that determines the appropriate *modus operandi* in the allocation of goods and bads. In particular, as such a perspective highlights, morality and inquiry are different enterprises that have very different aims and purposes in view.

A rather straightforward line of reflection emerges from these present considerations. Its starting point is the consideration—already emphasized in chapter 1 above—that credit allocation is generally a matter of established practice and custom. Now custom does not operate *in vacuo*; it generally has a rationale that is determined by the purposive nature of the practices at issue. And in consequence, share allocation—which in matters of distributive fairness runs in proportionate alignment with claims—will itself operate in a way that is dependent on customs that emerge from the purposive nature of the enterprise. The overall situation is accordingly deeply pragmatic. Fairness in division itself becomes a process that reflects the aims and purposes that are at issue in the context within which that division is made. And on this basis fairness itself can be seen in the light of a purposive instrumentality—one that is deeply entrenched in the ethical dimension of congenial human interaction.

Against this background, it is not hard to see that the different allocation processes at issue with moral and epistemic credit inhere in the functional goals of the enterprise at hand. For it emerges that this difference in comportment can be explained on the basis of the efficiency and effectiveness of those different modes of credit allocation in facilitating realization of the definitive goals and purposes operative in the respective domains.

Here even gambling affords an illustrative example. The proper principle of division of stakes in fair gambling is a matter of exact alignment with the actual or probable takings (wins or losses) of the parties at issue. And the reason for this principle is that fair access to winnings is the very reason for being of the enterprise at issue—the gambling enterprise. For it is the prospect of winning that motivates the participants here, and if this were not managed appropriately, people (that is sensible people) would be unwilling to enter into the venture. The whole enterprise would collapse for want of participation. And so here also it is the definitive aim of the enterprise that determines the proper modus operandi in matters of division.

Accordingly, the reality of it is that different rationales for allocating positivities and negativities are in order in different domains in line with the differences in aims and objectives of various human enterprises:

Ethics: To foster principles of interaction that induce people to act for the general welfare and the common good.

Law: To avert ways of action that damage the interests of others.

Scientific Inquiry: To advance the frontier of knowledge.

Gambling: To enable people to take calculated risks in ways that give them assured access to their winnings.

Politics: To facilitate the peaceful resolution of problems in the public domain.

However, while very different allocation principles are operative in different areas there is a uniform underlying rationale that accounts for these differences. For we have seen that in each case how it is that the characteristic and distinctive goal structure of the enterprise at issue determines how the distribution of positivities and negativities should properly function within its domain. Ultimately the rules of allocation are pragmatically rooted in the functional nature of the particular enterprise, attuned to and emergent from the characteristic teleology at issue. Like any deliberate activity, distribution has a definite function or aim. And the differences in *modus operandi* here all root in the variable requisites for achieving efficacy and effectiveness in realizing the particular characteristic aims of the enterprise at issue.

After all, even distributive fairness itself is a purposive project—one whose aim is to effect distributions in such a way that an intelligent bystander (an uninvolved third party) will have no occasion for endorsing a claimant's complaint that he has not been treated appropriately and that his allotted share is less than it properly and "by rights" ought to be. The allocation at issue has been effected in such a way that justice has been done and can be seen to have been done.

And so the issue of distributive appropriateness is ultimately not purely theoretical but pragmatic by way of hinging on considerations of purposive efficacy in the contexts at issue. For *the pragmatics regarding the functional teleology of an enterprise* both explains and validates its relevant allocation principles. Inquiry, morality, law, and the rest. represent particular sorts of human projects, each of which is characterized by a distinctive goal structure of ends, aims, and objectives of its own. And the cardinal rule of pragmatic rationality is uniformly the same throughout: "Proceed in a manner that is optimally efficient and effective in realizing the purposes at hand."[2] The *modus operandi* of allocation rules is rooted in just this purposive dimension of effectiveness and efficiency in goal-realization. And this consideration leads back to a key thesis of this book—that the subjectivistic approach to issues of fairness that has become commonplace in economics and decision theory fails to come to grips adequately with the fact that in matters of distributive justice one is dealing with a different purposive context where strictly ethical rather than merely practical considerations are paramount.

Notes

1. Some theorists maintain that there is such a thing as "moral luck," and that someone who runs risks of harming people are actually—but "unluckily" does harm has greater moral culpability than someone who runs the same risks but "gets away with it." Such theorists, however, confuse moral with legal culpability—as is all too common nowadays. (On these issues see Rescher 1995.)
2. What we have here is not an act-pragmatism ("Take that course of action which is optimally efficient and effective. . ."). Instead, its pragmatic thrust functions at the policy level because in the contingency of affairs individual outcomes are inherently less predictable than general tendencies. Observe that the situation is structurally much the same here as that of the act-utilitarianism vs. rule-utilitarianism conflict in moral theory.

Bibliography

Ackerman, Bruce A., *Social Justice in the Liberal State* (New Haven, CT: Yale University Press, 1980).
Alkan, Ahmet, Gabrielle Demange, and David Gale, "Fair Allocation of Indivisible Goods and Criteria of Justice," *Econometrica*, vol. 59 (1991), pp. 1023-40.
Aristotle, *Nicomachaen Ethics*, tr. W. D. Ross (Oxford: Oxford University Press, 1942).
Arneson, R, "Equality and Equal Opportunity for Welfare," *Philosophical Studies*, vol. 56 (1989), pp. 77-93.
Arnsperger, Christian, "Envy-Freeness and Distributive Justice," *Journal of Economic Studies*, vol. 21 (1994), pp. 155-86.
Arrow, Kenneth J., *Social Choice and Individual Values*, (New York: Wiley, 1951).
———, *Social Choice and Individual Values*, second ed. (New Haven, CT and London: Yale University Press, 1963).
Atkinson, Anthony B. and Joseph E. Stiglitz, *Lectures in Public Economics* (New York: McGraw Hill, 1980).
Baier, Kurt, "Maximization and Fairness," *Ethics*, vol. 96 (1985), pp. 119-29.
Balinski, Michel L. and H. Peyton Young, *Fair Representation: Meeting the Ideal of One Man, One Vote* (New Haven, CT: Yale University Press, 1982).
Barry, Brian M., *Theories of Justice* (London: Harvester Wheatsheaf, 1989).
———, *Justice as Impartiality* (Oxford: Clarendon Press, 1995).
Baumol, William J., *Superfairness: Applications and The*ory, (Cambridge, MA.: MIT Press, 1986).
Beck, Anatole, "Constructing a Fair Border," *American Mathematical Monthly*, vol. 94 (1987), pp. 157-162.
Billera, L. J., and D. C., Heath, "Allocation of Shared Costs: A Set of Axioms Yielding a Unique Procedure," *Mathematics of Operations Research*, vol. 7 (1982), pp. 32-39.
Ben-Ze'ev, Aaron, "Envy and Jealousy," *Canadian Journal of Philosophy*, vol 20 (1990), pp. 487-516.
———, "Envy and Inequality," *The Journal of Philosophy*, vol. 89 (1992), pp. 551-81.
Bergin, Thomas F., and Paul G. Haskell, *Preface to Estates in Land and Future Interests*, 2nd ed., *University Textbook Series* (Eagan, MN: Foundation Press, 1991).

Bers, S. A., and J. Rodin, "Social-Comparison Jealousy: A Developmental and Motivational Study," *Journal of Personality and Social Psychology*, vol. 47 (1984), pp. 766-79.

Bicchieri, Cristina, "Local Fairness," *Philosophy and Phenomenological Research*, vol. 59 (1999), pp. 229-34.

Binmore, Ken, *Game Theory and the Social Contract Volume I: Playing Fair* (Cambridge, MA.: MIT Press, 1994).

Brams, Steven J. and Alan D. Taylor, *Fair Division* (Cambridge: Cambridge University Press, 1996).

Broome, John, "Selecting People Randomly," *Ethics*, vol. 95 (1984), pp. 38-55.

———— "Fairness," *Proceedings of the Aristotelian Society*, Vol. LXXXXI (1990-91), pp. 87-101.

————, *Weighing Goods* (Oxford: Basil Blackwell, 1991).

Buchanan, Allen E., *Ethics, Efficiency, and the Market* (New York: Rowman and Allanheld, 1985).

Buchanan, James M. and Gordon Tullock *The Calculus of Consent* (Ann Arbor: University of Michigan Press, 1962).

Cahn, Edmond Nathaniel, *The Sense of Injustice: An Anthropocentric View of Law* (New York: New York University Press, 1949).

Carens, Joseph H., "Two Conceptions of Fairness: A Response to Veit Bader," *Political Theory*, vol. 25 (1997), pp. 814-20.

Champsaur, P., and G. Laroque, "Fair Allocations in Large Economics," *Journal of Economic Theory*, vol. 25 (1981), pp. 269-82.

Cicero, *De legibus*.

Cohen, G. A., "On the Currency of Egalitarian Justice," *Ethics*, vol. 99 (1989), pp. 906-44.

Cordero, Ronald A., "Aristotle and Fair Deals," *Journal of Business Ethics*, vol. 7 (1988), pp. 681-90.

Crawford, V. P., "A Game of Fair Division," *Review of Economic Studies*, vol. 44 (1977), pp. 235-47.

Crawford, V. P., and W. P. Heller, "Fair Division with Indivisible Commodities," *Journal of Economic Theory*, vol. 21 (1979), pp. 10-27.

Cupit, Geoffrey, "On the Injustice of Ignoring Entitlements," *Australasian Journal of Philosophy*, vol. 74 (1996), pp. 313-18.

Demange, Gabrielle, "Implementing Efficient Egalitarian Equivalent Allocations," *Econometrica*, vol. 52 (1984), pp. 1167-77.

Demko, Stephen and Theodore P. Hill, "Equitable Distribution of Indivisible Objects," *Mathematical Social Science*, vol. 16 (1988), pp. 1-14.

Diamantaras, D., "On Equity with Public Goods," *Social Choice and Welfare*, vol. 9 (1992), pp. 141-57.

Dubins, Lester E., "Group Decision Devices," *American Mathematical Monthly*, vol. 84 (1977), pp. 350-56.

Dubins, Lester E., and E. H., Spanier, "How to Cut a Cake Fairly," *American Mathematical Monthly*, vol. 68 (1961), pp. 1-17.

Dworkin, Ronald, *Sovereign Virtue: The Theory and Practice of Equality* (Cambridge, MA.: Harvard University Press, 2000).

Elster, Jon, "Taming Chance: Randomization in Judicial and Social Decisions," *Tanner Lectures on Human Values*, (Salt Lake City: University of Utah Press, 1988).
Feinberg, Joel, *Doing and Deserving* (Princeton, NJ: Princeton University Press, 1970).
Foley, D. K., "Resource Allocation in the Public Sector." *Yale Economic Essays*, No. 7 (New Haven Department of Economics: Yale University, 1967).
Folger, R., "Perceived Injustice, Referent Cognitions, and the Concept of Comparison Level," *Representative Research in Social Psychology*, vol. 14, (1984), pp. 88-108.
Frankfurt, Harry, "Equality as a Moral Ideal, in *The Importance of What We Care About* (Cambridge: Cambridge University Press, 1988).
Frey, Bruno S., and I. Bohnet, "Institutions affect Fairness: Experimental Investigations," *Journal of Institutional and Theoretical Economics*, vol. 151 (1995), pp. 286-303.
Frohlich, Norman and Joe Oppenheimer, *Choosing Justice: An Experimental Approach to Ethical Theory* (Berkeley: University of California Press, 1992).
Goldman, S. and C. Sussangkarn, "Dealing with Envy," *Journal of Economic Theory*, vol. 23 (1983), pp. 189-200.
Goodman, Barbara, *Justice by Lottery* (Chicago: University of Chicago Press, 1992).
Goodwin, William, *Political Justice* (Harmondsworth: Penguin Books, 1976).
Hart, W. D., "The Cake Problem," *Acta Philosophica Fennica*, vol. 38 (1985), pp. 25-35.
Hart, Herbert Lionel Adolphus and Antony Maurice Honore, *Causation in the Law* (Oxford: Clarendon Press, 1962).
Hill, Theodore P., "Determining a Fair Border," *American Mathematical Monthly*, vol. 90 (1983), pp. 438-42.
———, "Mathematical Devices for Getting a Fair Share," *American Scientist*, vol. 88 (2000), pp. 325-31.
Hively, Will, "Dividing the Spoils", *Discover*, vol. 16 (July, 1995), pp. 49-57.
Holcombe, J. H., "Applied Fairness Theory: A Comment," *American Economic Review*, vol. 73 (1983), pp. 1153-56.
Hurwicz, Leonid, David Schmeidler, and Hugo Sonnenschein (eds.) *Social Goals and Social Organization: Essays in Memory of Elisha Pazner* (Cambridge: Cambridge University Press, 1985).
Jolowicz, H. F., *Historical Introduction to the Study of Roman Law*, end ed. (Cambridge: Cambridge University Press, 1952).
Kahneman, Daniel, J. Knetsch, and R. Thaler, "Fairness as a Constraint on Profit Seeking: Entitlements in the Market," *American Economic Review*, vol. 76 (1986), pp. 728-41.
Keynes, J. M., *A Treatise on Probability* (London: Methuen, 1921).
Knaster, Bronislaw, "Sur le problème du partage pragmatique de H. Steinhaus" *Annales de le Societé Polanaise Mathematique*, vol. 19 (1946), pp. 228-30.

Knaster, Bronislaw and H. Steinhaus, "Sur le partage pragmatique," *Compies Rendus de la Societé des Sciences et des Lettres de Wroclaw*, Communications 1 and 2 (1953).

Kolm, Serge-Christophe, *Justice et Equité* (Paris: Editions du CNRS, 1972).

———, *Modern Theories of Justice* (Cambridge, MA.: MIT Press, 1996).

Kuhn, H. W., "On Games of Fair Division," in M. Shubik (ed.), *Essays in Mathematical Economics in Honor of Oskar Morgenstern* (Princeton, 1967), pp. 29-37.

Le Grand, Julian, *Equity and Choice: An Essay in Economics and Applied Philosophy*, (Bristol: Harper Collins, 1991).

Legut, Jerzy. "The Problem of Fair Division for Countably Many Participants," *Journal of Mathematica Analysis Applied*, vol. 109 (1985), pp. 83-89.

———, "A Game of Fair Division with Continuum of Players," *Colloquia Mathematica*, vol. 53 (1987), pp. 323-31.

———, "On Totally Balanced Games Arising From Cooperation in Fair Division," *Games and Economic Behavior*, vol. 2 (1990), pp. 47-60.

Leibniz, G. W., *Juris ac aequi elementa,* in *Mitteilungen aus Leibnizens ungedruckten Schriften*, ed. G. Mollat (Leipzig: H. Haessel, 1893).

Lensberg, Terje, "Bargaining and Fair Allocation," in *Cost Allocation: Methods, Principles, Applications* H. Peyton Young (ed.), (North Holland: Elsevier Science Publishers, 1985), pp. 101-116.

Locke, John, *Essays Concerning Human Understanding*.

Luce, R. Duncan and Howard Raiffa, *Games and Decisions* (New York: John Wiley & Sons, 1957).

Maskin, Eric S. (ed.), "On the Fair Allocation of Indivisible Goods," in *Arrow and the Foundations of the Theory of Economic Policy* (1987), pp. 341-9.

Massey, Gerald, "Tom, Dick, Harry, and All the King's Men," *American Philosophical Quarterly*, vol. 13 (1976), pp. 89-107.

Mora, Gonzalo Fernández de la, *Egalitarian Envy: The Political Foundations of Social Justice* (New York: Paragon House Publishers, 1987).

Moulin, Hever, "Fair Divisions Under Joint Ownership: Recent Results and Open Problems," *Social Choice and Welfare*, vol. 7 (1990), pp. 149-70.

Moulin, Herve, and Scott Shenker, "Serial Cost Sharing," *Econometrica*, vol. 60 (1992), pp. 1009-37.

Nozick, Robert, *Anarchy, State, and Utopia* (New York: Basic Books, 1974).

Okun, Arthur M., *Equality and Efficiency: The Big Tradeoff* (Washington, DC.: Brookings Institution, 1975).

Plato, *Republic*.

Pratt, John Winsor and Richard Jay Zeckhauser, "The Fair and Efficient Division of the Winsor Family Silver," *Management Science*, vol. 36, (1990), pp. 1293-1301.

Rabin, Matthew, "Incorporating Fairness into Game Theory and Economics," *American Economic Review*, vol. 83 (1993), pp. 1281-1302.

Rabinovitz, Nachum L., *Probability and Statistical Inference in Ancient and Medieval Jewish Literature* (Toronto: Demand Books UMI, 1973).

Rawls, John, "Justice as Fairness" *The Philosophical Review*, vol. 67 (1958), pp. 164-94.

———, *A Theory of Justice* (Cambridge, MA: Harvard University Press, 1971).
Rescher, Nicholas, *Distributive Justice* (New York: Bobbs-Merrill, 1966).
———, "A Kantian Conception of Equality," *Cambridge Review*, February 1975, pp. 94-99.
———, "The Allocation of Exotic Medical Lifesaving Therapy," *Ethics*, vol. 79 (1969), pp. 173-86.
———, *Risk: A Philosophical Introduction to the Theory of Risk Evaluation and Management* (Washington, DC: University Press of America, 1983).
———, "Leibniz, Keynes, and the Rabbis on a Problem of Distributive Justice," *The Journal of Philosophy*, vol. 86 (1989), pp. 337-52.
———, *Luck* (New York: Farrar, Straus & Giroux, 1995).
Roemer, John E., *Egalitarian Perspectives: Essays in Philosophical Economics* (Cambridge: Cambridge University Press, 1994).
Ross, William David, *Aristotle*, 5th edn. (London: Routledge, 1964).
Runciman, Walter Garrison, *Relative Deprivation and Social Justice* (London: Routledge and Kegan Paul, 1966).
Salovey, Peter, *The Psychology of Jealousy and Envy* (New York: Guilford, 1991).
Samuels, W. J. and N., Mercuro, "Property Rights, Equity, and Public Utility Pricing," in *New Dimensions in Public Utility Pricing* (East Lansing: Division of Research of Michigan State University, 1976).
Samuelson, W., "Dividing Coastal Waterways," *Journal of Conflict Resolution*, vol. 29 (1985), pp. 83-111.
Schmeidler, David and Karl Vind, "Fair Net Trades," *Econometrica*, vol. 40 (1972), pp. 637-42.
Selten, R., "The Equity Principle in Economic Behavior," in H. W. Gottinger and W. Leingelner (eds.), *Decision Theory and Social Ethics: Issues in Social Choice* (Dordrecht: Reidel, 1978), pp. 289-301.
Sen, Amartya K., *Collective Choice and Social Welfare* (San Francisco: Holden-Day, 1970).
———, *On Econimic Equiality* (Oxford: Oxford University Press, 1973).
———, "Equality of What?," in S. McMurrin (ed.), *The Tanner Lectures on Human Values*, vol. 1, (Cambridge: Cambridge University Press, 1980).
———, *Inequality Reexamined* (Cambridge, MA.: Harvard University Press, 1992).
Sher, George, "What Makes a Lottery Fair?," *Nous*, vol. 14 (1980), pp. 203-14.
Sidgwick, Henry, *The Methods of Ethics*, 7th edn., (London: Macmillan, 1907).
Smith, Adam, *The Theory of Moral Sentiments*.
———, *The Wealth of Nations*.
Steinhaus, Hugo, "The Problem of Fair Division," *Econometrica*, vol. 16 (1948), pp. 101-04.
———, "Sur la division pragmatique," *Econometrica* vol. 17 (1949), supplement, pp. 315-19.
Stone, A. H., and J. W. Tukey, "Generalized 'Sandwich' Theorems," *Duke Mathematical Journal*, vol. 9 (1942), pp. 356-59.
Stromquist, W., "How to Cut a Cake Fairly," *American Mathematical Monthly* vol. 87 (1980), pp. 640-44.

Svensson, L. G., "Large Indivisibilities: An Analysis with Respect to Price Equalibria and Fairness," *Econometrica*, vol. 51 (1983), pp. 939-54.
———, "On the Existence of Fair Allocations," *Journal of Economics*, vol. 43 (1983), pp. 301-8
Sverdlik, Steven, "The Logic of Desert," *Journal of Value Inquiry*, vol. 17 (1983), p. 323.
Thomson, W., "An Informationally Efficient Equality Criterion," *Journal of Public Economics*, vol. 18 (1983), pp. 243-63.
———, "The Fair Division of a Fixed Supply Among a Growing Population," *Mathematics of Operations Research*, vol., 1 (1983), pp. 319-26.
———, "Problems of Fair Division and the Egalitarian Solution," *Journal of Economic Theory*, vol. 31 (1983), pp. 211-26.
Thomson, W., and H. Varian, "Theories of Justice Based on Symmetry," in Hurwicz, Schmeidler, and Sonnenschein (eds.), (1985).
Tuomela, Raimo, *Cooperation* (Dordrecht: Kluwer, 2000).
Varian, Hal R,, "Envy, Equity, and Efficiency," *Journal of Economic Theory*, vol. 9 (1974), pp. 63-91.
———, "Distributive Justice, Welfare Economics, and the Theory of Justice," *Journal of Philosophy and Public Affairs*, vol. 4 (1975), pp. 223-47.
———, "Two Problems in the Theory of Fairness," *Journal of Public Economics* vol. 5 (1976), pp. 249-60.
Vohra, R., "Equity and Efficiency in Non-convex Economics," *Social Choice and Welfare*, vol. 9 (1992), pp. 185-202.
Waller, Bruce N., "Uneven Starts and Just Deserts," *Analysis*, vol. 49 (1989), pp. 209-213.
Walster, Elaine, G. William Walster, and Ellen Berscheid,, *Equity: Theory and Research* (Boston: Allyn and Bacon, 1979).
Walzer, Michael, *Spheres of Justice* (Oxford, Oxford University Press, 1983).
Weber, Max, *Economy and Society*, ed. by G. Roth and C. Wittick (Berkeley & Los Angeles: University of California Press, 1988).
Weingartner, H. Martin, and Bezalel Gavish, "How to Settle an Estate," *Management Science*, vol. 39, (1993), pp. 588-601.
Woodall, D. R., "Dividing a Cake Fairly," *Journal of Mathematical Analysis Applied*, vol. 78 (1980), pp. 233-47.
Yaari, Menahem E., "Rawls, Edgeworth, Shapley, Nash: Theories of Distributed Justice Re-examined," *Journal of Economic Theory*, vol. 24 (1981), pp. 1-39.
Yaari, Menahem and M. Bar-Hillel, "On Dividing Justly," *Social Choice and Welfare*, vol. 1 (1984), pp. 1-24.
Young, H. Peyton, (ed.), *Cost Allocation: Methods, Principles, Applications* (North Holland: Elsevier Science Publishers, 1985).
———, "On Dividing an Amount Accordingly to Individual Claims or Liabilities," *Mathematical Operations Res*earch, vol. 12 (1987), pp. 398-414.
———, "Fair Division" in idem (ed.), *Negotiation Analysis* (Ann Arbor: University of Michigan Press, 1991), pp. 25-45.
———, *Equity* (Princeton, NJ: Princeton University Press, 1992).

Young, Robert, Egalitarianism and Envy," *Philosophical Studies*, vol. 52 (1987), pp. 261-76.

Zajac, Edward E., *Fairness or Efficiency: An Introduction to Public Utility Pricing* (Cambridge, MA.: Ballinger, 1978).

———, "Perceived Economic Justice: The Example of Public Utility Regulation," in Young 1985.

Name Index

Aristotle, 1, 16, 22, 24n1, 24n17, 62, 85, 102n5
Asher ben Yehiel, Rabbi, 95
Atkinson, Anthony B., 24n6

Balinski, Michael L., 43n11
Bana, Rabbi, 95
Barry, Brian, M., 24n15
Baumol, William J., 43n4, 79n2
Bergin, Thomas, F., 110n4
Bernoulli, David, 89n3
Brams, Steven J., 24n7, 24n13, 43n10, 54n1, 80n3, 80n4, 80n5, 102n8
Broome, John, 24n2, 24n5, 43n9, 90n12, 102n10
Butler, Bishop, 85

Carnap, Rudolf, 119
Cicero, 93
Couturat, Louis, 90n9

D'Alembert, Jean, 89n3
Daston, Lorrain, 89n 4
de Méré, Chevalier, 83
De Witt, Pensionary, 83, 89n4

Ehrenfest, Paul, 80n2
Elster, Jon, 90n12, 102n6
Epstein, Richard A., 102n1

Feldman, Allan, 43n4
Foley, D. K., 43n4, 79n2

Goldman, Alvin, 110n1
Goodman, Barbara, 43n7, 43n8

Hart, H. L. A., 24n4
Hart, W. D., 24n7, 43n6
Haskell, Paul G., 110n4
Hill, Theodore P., 43n6
Honoré, A. M., 24n4

Hospers, John, 24n12
Hull, David, 110n1
Huygens, M., 83, 89n4

Jolowicz, H. F., 24n3

Kant, Immanuel, 24n12, 116
Kerman, Alan, 43n4
Keynes, John Maynard, 43n4, 81, 83, 86, 87, 88, 89, 89n2, 89n6, 90n12, 91, 92, 97, 101, 102n2, 119
Knaster, Bronislaw, 79n1, 80n3

Laudan, Larry, 110n1
Leibniz, G. W., 81-89, 89n1, 89n2, 89n3, 89n4, 89n5, 90n10, 90n11, 92, 93, 97, 101, 119
Locke, John, 90n8
Luce, R. Duncan, 80n4

Mandeville, Bernard de, 79
Massey, Gerald, 110n2

Pascal, Balise, 45, 89n4
Pascal, M., 83
Pazner, Elisha, 79n2
Placcius, Vincentius, 81
Plato, 16, 24n9

Rabinovitz, Nachum, 102n7
Raiffa, Howard, 80n4
Rawls, John, 102n11
Roemer, John, 43n4
Ross, W. D., 24n11

Sen, Amartya K., 43n4
Shaked, Moshe, 110n1
Sidgwick, Henry, xii, xiiin1, 25, 26, 43n1
Simonides, 16
Smith, Adam, 31

Solomon, King, 93
Spanier, E. H., 24n7
Steinhaus, Hugo, 79n1
Stiglitz, Joseph E ., 24n6

Taylor, 24n7, 24n13, 43n10, 54n1, 80n3, 80n4, 80n5, 102n8
Thomson, W. 43n4
Tuomela, Raimo, 110n3

Varian, Hal R., 43n4, 79n2

Wagner, Gabriel, 89n1
Weber, Max, 21, 24n16
Wolff, Jonathan, 43n12

Yaari, Menahem, 79n2
Young, H, Peyton, 43n11